CHRISTIAN VOLUNTARISM

FAITH'S HORIZONS

RONALD E. VALLET
general editor

Stepping Stones of the Steward, second edition
Ronald E. Vallet

The Mainline Church's Funding Crisis
Ronald E. Vallet and Charles E. Zech

Christian Voluntarism
William H. Brackney

Other volumes forthcoming

CHRISTIAN VOLUNTARISM

Theology and Praxis

WILLIAM H. BRACKNEY

WILLIAM B. EERDMANS PUBLISHING COMPANY
GRAND RAPIDS, MICHIGAN / CAMBRIDGE, U.K.

REV/ROSE PUBLISHING
MANLIUS, NEW YORK

© 1997 by REV/Rose Ministries, Inc.

Published by Wm. B. Eerdmans Publishing Co.
255 Jefferson Ave. S.E., Grand Rapids, Michigan 49503 /
P.O. Box 163, Cambridge CB3 9PU U.K.
All rights reserved

Printed in the United States of America

02 01 00 99 98 97   7 6 5 4 3 2 1

Library of Congress Cataloging-in-Publication Data

Brackney, William H.
Christian voluntarism : theology and praxis / William H. Brackney.
p.   cm. — (Faith's horizons)
Includes bibliographical references and index.
ISBN 0-8028-0863-8 (paper : alk. paper)
1. Voluntarism — Religious aspects — Christianity. I. Title. II. Series.
BR115.V64B73   1997
267 — dc21   96-40522
CIP

For
George C. Lurwick
My first mentor in Christian ministry
and
John W. Irwin
Whose dedication to voluntary Christianity
has been a model

Contents

CONTENTS

The Faith's Horizons Series and Christian Voluntarism

The purpose of the Faith's Horizons series is to explore factors affecting the church and to find places of hope and leverage points of change. To accomplish this purpose, the series seeks to provide information, analysis, theological reflection, and insights to assist church leaders, both lay and clergy, in understanding and responding faithfully to the foundational shift that is affecting the church in North America and in other parts of the world.

The church as *a household of faith* is a setting for nurture and sustenance — both physical and spiritual. The church too often forgets that it *is* a community of faith, however. Metaphors of management and psychological therapy control and even overwhelm the call to the church to be a faithful, hopeful, loving community.

The *horizon* is the line where the sky seems to meet the earth. As such, it is the boundary between the visible and the invisible — the seen and the unseen. The word "horizon" is a reminder that a change of position or perspective can bring a view not seen before. With new views can come insights. Even more, beyond the horizon, a new vision beckons people of faith.

The series' name, Faith's Horizons, refers to the members of the household of faith as they seek new understandings and perspectives — new horizons — and is based on these four *assumptions:* (1) The church is moving into uncharted territory — where the horizon is shifting. (Some have described this as a postmodern age.) (2) There is confusion and denial about what is happening in the church and why it is happening. (3) In its new situation, the church is called to be countercultural. (4) God provides hope for the church.

The series seeks to be on the cutting edge of the life of the church and, consequently, may take positions and stances that are untraditional and not popular. This is done with a deep sense of caring and love for the world that God created and loves. The call of faithful Christians to be stewards of the mysteries of God is deeply imbedded within the ethos of the series.

It is not a series of "how to's." Instead, it attempts to deal with where we are coming from and to raise a vision of where we are headed — and why. A challenge to commitment and risk taking is an integral part of the series.

Sometimes, to gain a clearer understanding/view of what lies ahead, it is important to look at the road that has brought us to the point where we are now. On the subject of Christian voluntarism, we could have no better guide than William H. Brackney, principal of McMaster Divinity College, Hamilton, Ontario. Dr. Brackney, who is a distinguished church historian, has studied and written about voluntarism over a number of years.

Christian Voluntarism: Theology and Praxis first looks at the biblical backgrounds and the theological bases of Christian voluntarism. This is followed by an in-depth historical perspective on Christian voluntarism over the centuries, focussing on the experience of Christian voluntarism in Britain and North America. The emerging evolutionary patterns of Christian voluntarism are also described in Part One.

The second part of the book deals with the praxis of Christian voluntarism and examines how religious voluntary associations work and the interrelationships and interactions between the church and parachurch. An entire chapter is devoted to the critical role of voluntarism within the Christian congregation.

In a day when congregations and denominations report ongoing shortages of enough resources to do their work, it is both refreshing and exciting to be reminded of the experience of the Israelites in the wilderness when Moses had to restrain God's people from bringing more gifts for God's work because "what they had already brought was more than enough to do all the work" (Exod. 36:7).

Surprisingly, little has been written before about voluntarism within the Christian congregation. Dr. Brackney's contribution in this chapter is significant. The interplay between voluntary decisions made by individual members of the congregation on the one hand and what it means to make vows and to be part of a covenanted community on the other hand is an important subject. It particularly comes into play in the observances of baptism and communion.

In the final chapter, Dr. Brackney lists some of the enduring values of Christian voluntarism and details what voluntarism suggests for the future. His specific suggestions about what is needed in the late twentieth and early twenty-first centuries are helpful and point to new vistas of faith's horizons.

Ronald E. Vallet
General Editor
Faith's Horizons Series

Foreword

Finally, the story is told. The history of Christianity is in its voluntarism. Without it, congregations, denominations, and religious associations could not exist. Furthermore, voluntarism is at the very essence — the very meaning — of communities of faith. *Christian Voluntarism* by William Brackney is a wonderfully informative book. Its subtitle is "Theology and Praxis." This volume reviews the *theology* from which voluntarism in the Christian tradition emerged and has been reinterpreted over the centuries. The *praxis* involves a history and reflective discussion of the practice of voluntarism in churches, religious associations, and, in a more recent organizational form, the parachurch organization. While voluntary action emanating from religious institutions has been discussed by other historians, this is the first time that the focus of a volume is on the meaning and practice of voluntarism within the church. The message of this volume, if any, is that practitioners in the church need to remember their roots, and that the energy of congregations comes from spiritual engagement and *doing good works*. For it is in the doing that faith is acted out.

In my experience, very few laypeople understand how congregations function and the absolute importance and necessity of their participation. From the surveys conducted by INDEPENDENT SECTOR of the activities of congregations in the United States, it is clear that religious institutions would close down without the voluntary participation of members of congregations, from working in all areas of church activities to serving the church in the community. Over

90 percent of all persons working in congregations are volunteers, and 60 percent of all hours worked are provided by volunteers. When I talked to volunteers from congregations, they were astounded with these findings. No one had told them how important their leadership and participation are to the life of a church and to its work in the community and the world. It is a well-kept secret. I suspect that very few sermons deal with voluntarism and its relation to faith and good works. The most common story told about voluntary help is the "Good Samaritan."

Brackney provides some very good stories about voluntary action and the formation of voluntary religious associations in both the Old and New Testaments. But the story he provides for the foundation of the structure of Christianity and its subsequent institutional forms reminds me why members of congregations may understand the voluntary and communal spirit of the Christian faith far better than many representatives of the institutional church do. The story of the first association formed informally at Christ's Last Supper with his twelve disciples and its formal establishment at Pentecost is a strong reminder that the original church was a voluntary religious association. The early Christians who had taken on a voluntary commitment to become Christians served each other and the disciples to build community. One need only visit the Church of the Nativity in Bethlehem and the Church of the Holy Sepulchre in Jerusalem to understand the communal nature of early Christianity.

Brackney also shows how Christianity became institutionalized in Continental Europe and Great Britain and how monastic orders carried on the tradition of voluntarism in a large institutionalized church. But it really was the Protestant Reformation and particularly the growth of the Nonconformists in Great Britain that inspired the development of numerous independent churches and denominations in the colonies. Thanks to Erasmus and John Locke, immigrants to the colonies wrote a United States Constitution that separated church and state. Thus, the church in the United States became a voluntary association. As such, religious institutions from all faiths grew and prospered there. Great revivals and evangelical movements in both Great Britain and North America led to missions abroad, to the creation of institutions and associations, including again, thanks to the volunteers, the creation of denominations and ecumenical organizations, such as the American Bible Society, the great antislavery societies, and the women's suffrage movement. In each of these revivals, it was laypeople who exercised their faith in trying to eradicate injustice and to create schools and colleges, hospitals, orphanages, and a plethora of voluntary social service organizations.

More recently, the Christian evangelical movement has created organizations, such as the Christian Coalition, to influence politics. Brackney concludes that the tradition of religious voluntarism, especially as it developed in America, greatly broadened participation and involvement of average people in Christian activities. He argues that such associations can motivate more individuals to participate. His recommendation to clergy is that such efforts need to be harnessed and encouraged if congregations are to remain vital. I think the message is long overdue.

As Brackney looks at the creation of very successful parachurch organizations, such as World Vision, and the downsizing of large national denominational offices, he wonders about the health of the church at the congregational level. But throughout history, he notes, one can see the revitalization of the congregations and the creation of new organizations that inspire local communities of faith that want to do good works. Individuals want to become actively engaged in their faith and to rebuild community. If the congregation works on such outreach, it will probably be renewed through the energy of its lay members. I hope this book is on the required reading lists of both laypeople and the clergy. It speaks well to the future and suggests rich avenues for congregational and denominational renewal.

Virginia A. Hodgkinson
Vice President for Research
INDEPENDENT SECTOR
and Georgetown University
Washington, D.C.

Introduction

As part of the "Faith's Horizons" series, this book seeks to understand better the voluntary nature of the church and Christian mission. In a pluralistic and voluntaristic culture, such as much of that in the West, it is of the highest priority to relate the Christian message to social realities. Freedom of human expression and opportunity, the value of the individual, democratic decision making, and the organizational shifts from a clergy-dominant church to a church of lay initiative all suggest the relevance of voluntarism. It is not overstating the case to argue that all Christian churches have been transformed by the voluntary impulse in the past three centuries. Theologically, the Christian community must comprehend and develop a suitable apologetic for this reality.

So, what is voluntarism and precisely how has it shaped our understanding of the faith? And, more importantly, how can a better understanding of voluntarism improve our self-understanding as a faithful people and our involvement in discipleship and mission?

To begin with, a definition of terms is in order. "Voluntary" is derived from *voluntas*, meaning "will." By voluntarism is meant that which is characterized by the freedom of the will. Single acts may be characterized as "voluntary," and when persons cooperate of their own free choice to accomplish a task or objective a "voluntary association" may result.[1] Voluntary associations contrast with other

---

1. Definitions are not simple among social scientists. As Jerry G. Bode has shown, there is a history to defining "voluntary associations." See his helpful

social institutions like the family, government, school, and the military, where membership is involuntary or involves coercion. Recent sociological analysis has circumscribed a *voluntary* or "third sector" of societies between the "state" and the "market," where activities are free of formal coercion and the economic constraints of profitability.[2] Some voluntary associations in this sector may be informal and temporary, while others may take on permanent character and even become institutionalized, or what social scientists refer to as "formal voluntary associations."[3] It is part of human nature to associate, and voluntary associations provide cultures with important functions like social integration, distribution of power, and training in necessary skills. Religion provides a powerful incentive to associate, and this is witnessed in most of the world's major religions. In the Christian context, voluntary associations have had a similarly profound impact upon the meaning and function of church and mission. As voluntary associations in general provide a "filling and connective tissue" between major social structures and between individuals and structures, so religious associations provide connective social tissue between the individual and the church and in some instances between religious structures.[4]

---

chapter "The Voluntary Association Concept in Twentieth Century American Sociology," in David Horton Smith, ed., *Voluntary Action Research: 1972* (New York: D. C. Heath, 1972), 53-619. See also the series of essays in *Voluntary Associations,* ed. J. Roland Pennock and John W. Chapman (New York: Atherton Press, 1969), for political and legal aspects.

2. David Horton Smith and Burt R. Baldwin, "Voluntary Associations and Volunteering in the United States," in *Voluntary Action Research 1974: The Nature of Voluntary Action Around the World,* ed. David Horton Smith (Lexington, Mass.: Lexington Books, 1974), 277-83; Max L. Stackhouse, "Religion and the Social Space for Voluntary Institutions," in *Faith and Philanthropy: Exploring the Role of Religion in America's Voluntary Sector,* ed. Robert Wuthnow and Virginia A. Hodgkinson (San Francisco: Jossey Bass, 1990), ch. 2; Robert Wuthnow, ed., *Between States and Markets: The Voluntary Sector in Comparative Perspective* (Princeton, N.J.: Princeton University Press, 1991), 7.

3. Bartolomeo J. Palisi, "A Critical Analysis of the Voluntary Association Concept," *Sociology and Social Research,* 52 (July 1968): 392-405.

4. For a definition of voluntary associations in religious context, compare the articles "Voluntarism," in *The Westminster Dictionary of Church History,* ed.

Introduction

Christian voluntarism began as an idea, a philosophic and theological construct, and gradually made its way into experience. One means of discovering the foundation of Christian voluntarism is to identify the course of Judeo-Christian thought that emphasized spontaneity of action in the religious community. Related to this phenomenon is an ethical mandate, the "need to do good works" in the communities of faith in various stages of Israel's history and later the Christian Church. For some, the idea of *caritas,* derived from the Ten Commandments and Christ's two great commandments, undergirds the definition of a Christian society and fraternal cooperation and provides an important foundational construct.[5] Because a theological community is by its nature constantly reflective, the debate over human initiative and benevolence occupied much attention in the life of the Christian church for two-thirds of its recorded history.

Yet another strategy is to identify the contextual social and organizational realities that influenced specifically Christian voluntarism: the evolution of patterns of benevolence and the growth of various kinds of associations. One might well look at how the sick were cared for or how workers' guilds and fraternal associations influenced the Christian churches. In these cases, it is possible to argue that theological definition was in fact shaped by praxis.

This book is concerned with both of these foundations of Christian voluntarism — the theoretical and the practical — and more. The implications of Christian voluntarism for the organized churches and other forms of Christian endeavour, like the twentieth-century parachurch organization, are limitless. Beyond historical

---

Jerald C. Brauer (Philadelphia: The Westminster Press, 1971), 852-53; "Voluntaryism, Voluntarism," in *Dictionary of Christianity in America,* ed. Daniel J. Reid (Downers Grove, Ill.: InterVarsity Press, 1990), 1227-28; "Voluntaryism," in *Encyclopedic Dictionary of Religion,* vol. 3, ed. Paul Kevin Meagher et al. (Washington, D.C.: Corpus Publications, 1979), 3692-93; and "Voluntarism, Baptist Views of," in *The Dictionary of Baptists in America,* ed. Bill J. Leonard (Downers Grove, Ill.: InterVarsity Press, 1994), 279-80.

5. R. N. Swanson, *Religion and Devotion in Europe, c. 1215–c. 1515* (Cambridge: Cambridge University Press, 1995), 18-19, 206-8.

analysis must come some reflection on the contemporary shapes of voluntarism as well as how voluntary associations behave. Finally, one can wonder what the enduring values of voluntarism might be. Properly understood, can this energy be harnessed practically in a theologically acceptable form?

It was several years ago now that I heard a leading historian describe his understanding of the English Nonconformist movement in the early seventeenth century as essentially voluntary churches: "If it wasn't voluntary," he asserted, "it wasn't a true church at all." That comment was the beginning of my own search for what voluntary Christianity means and implies. Within my own tradition, I found that many believed voluntariness was a quality that belonged to a particular denominational tradition. Upon further investigation, however, I found that the voluntary impulse is as old as Scripture and as broad as Christianity. In fact, radical Protestants of the fifteenth century and later simply recovered an ancient fiber of our faith and accentuated it.

In the dream and making of this work many people have been helpful. Dr. Noel Brann, an undergraduate professor of history, introduced me to the work of Pico della Mirandola; B. Burns Brodhead showed me when I was a seminary student the variety of those in the Methodist persuasion; F. Ernest Stoeffler in graduate school plumbed the depths of the Puritan and Pietist experiences in Europe and North America; Robert T. Handy's published work and his personal insights helped me to see the importance in the American religious experience of the voluntary association, as did J. K. Zeman in the Canadian context. James E. Berney of Inter-Varsity Canada has been a valued friend and source of data. Outside North America I have received invaluable assistance from David Lagergren, John H. Y. Briggs, and B. R. White. My friend and researcher, Dr. David Doherty of Hayling Island, Hants., has provided important assistance on matters relating to Great Britain. As a denominational staff person, I learned from Robert C. Campbell and Richard Gladden the tension between autonomy and interdependence, and I especially profited from Paul Harrison's seminal work, *Authority and Power in the Free Church Tradition* (1959). My faculty colleagues at McMaster Divinity College have also been very generous with critique and suggestions, especially Clark Pinnock, Reinhold Kerstan, Joyce Bellous, William Wood, Ruth Fraser, and Ken Bellous. Associate Dean Malcolm Horsnell's insights into biblical evidences of voluntarism were most helpful. As always, the library staff at Mills Library, McMaster University, has satisfied my appetite for resources and details. Mrs. Terri Galan, administrative secretary in the principal's office, provided the always-necessary technical assistance. A very special word of gratitude is due Dr. Ronald Vallet, who encouraged the inclusion of the idea in this series and who has been a flexible and thoughtful editor.

To all others who helped me and supported this project, especially the trustees of McMaster Divinity College, I express my sincere appreciation.

William H. Brackney
Christmastide 1996

"Only God's Spirit gives new life. The Spirit is like the wind that blows wherever it wants to. You can hear the wind but you don't know where it comes from or where it is going."

Jesus of Nazareth to Nicodemus, a ruler of the Jews

Meet Two Friends . . .
Two Perspectives

I have two composite friends who represent two very different approaches to Christian faithfulness. Their orientations speak vividly of the times in which we live.

My first friend, David, is a lifelong clergyman. He was reared in a pastor's home, nurtured in the churchly Christian experiences of the 1950s and 1960s. He attended a church-related college and then, in response to a call to ministry, attended a denominational theological seminary. Later he completed his doctoral degree in ministry, and he has served in several churches as a full-time pastor across Canada for over twenty years. He expects to retire in his mid-sixties from this kind of ministry.

David appreciates classical music and plays the organ. His taste in worship is slightly formal and best described as "traditional." His worship services feature a modest amount of liturgy, and he depends on a good, well-practised choir. His preaching is usually descriptive and mildly convictional, and he considers himself "ecumenical" in the cooperatively denominational sense of that term. My friend is very concerned that denominational standards for ministry be maintained, and he believes he can demonstrate a troubling diminution of concern for propriety and denominational ethos. It is fair to say that David is threatened by "parachurch Christianity," which he thinks robs his church of needed dollars for legitimate mission programmes. He also finds that people in the parachurch maintain a skepticism about the established church, and he is turned off by their "churchy" language.

David is married to a childhood girlfriend who quite actively supports his pastoral ministry. She is president of the Woman's Christian Service Guild and is past president of the denomination's ladies' organization. David and his wife have three children and are proud of their children's choices to follow their father in attending David's college.

My second friend is a woman named Laura who has an earned doctorate in natural sciences. She, too, was raised in a Christian home, somewhat on the conservative evangelical side, in the 1940s and 1950s. In her undergraduate years she became involved in the InterVarsity movement and other Christian organizations. She has taught science in a Christian college for over two decades. She is a member of the American Scientific Affiliation and is dedicated to interpreting her scientific hypotheses in light of her Christian values. She is married to a man who operates a small business, and their children attend a private Christian high school.

Laura is an indefatigable Christian worker. She is a member of the Bible society board and the local chapter of InterVarsity, and she campaigns for World Vision when it launches a special emphasis. She is a member of a cell group that is actively involved in prayer and Bible study, and she speaks often of her "spiritual" ministries as a volunteer. Laura is active in her church, which is a large regional congregation composed of mostly young, upwardly professional people and which supports a variety of mission programmes. Laura can be critical of organized religion as "stale and formal, lacking in spirit and vitality." She uses her musical talent as part of the worship team that performs on Sunday mornings in the school gymnasium where the church meets. In the course of Laura's many household moves and searches for the best congregational home for her family, she and her husband have been members of three denominations and five churches. She believes she is essentially ecumenical in maintaining close friendships with Roman Catholics and Jewish believers.

These two friends represent for me the most significant divergences in North American and British religious attitudes in this generation. Similar backgrounds, different pilgrimages, and much different relationships. Often my friends are at counterpoint with each other and me. Sometimes our differences are so deeply felt that our friendships depend on avoidance of conversation focussed on religious matters. With this kind of differentiation in the contemporary Christian community, there is a serious debate about what style of Christian endeavour meets the needs of the Christian faith in this generation; and beyond all else, what orientation is most desirable to the professing Christian community?

Both David and Laura exhibit voluntarist tendencies, that is, they are anxious to be active in the things of God and they willingly and spontaneously contribute their time and talent and resources to the cause of Christ. The roots and foundations of their voluntarism, as well as their separate identities, present the need for a better understanding of the theology and praxis of Christian voluntarism. The chapters that follow examine this important phenomenon.

PART I

BACKGROUNDS

CHAPTER ONE

Biblical Backgrounds of Christian Voluntarism

I. Old Testament Illustrations

While examples of voluntary association for religious purposes are lacking in any formal sense in the history of Israel before the Christian era, there are interesting examples of voluntary behaviour that suggest both social and theological themes. What must be avoided is the easy tendency to translate modern social phenomena back into ancient historical contexts and vice versa. In biblical exegesis, one must respect the incompleteness of the data to illustrate modern phenomena, while also recognizing the legitimate literary and religious objectives of various writers and editors who created our perceptions of the theological community over many centuries.

There are several instances of people organizing themselves voluntarily for a religious purpose in the history of Israel. Some were positive contributions, while others bore negatively on the community. One fascinating countercultural example was the Aaronic-inspired movement among the wandering tribes in Sinai. While Moses was receiving the law on the mountain, impatience with his leadership and his lengthy absence from the community led a group to organize themselves spontaneously to create an object of worship, the golden calf. There is a paucity of evidence about what actually happened, but one may assume from the text in Exodus 32 that an informal association gathered around Aaron, asking him "to make

9

gods for us, to go before us" (32:1). Once the golden calf was created, which presumably took some days, there was eating, drinking, and merrymaking (Exod. 32:6), in other words, reinforcement of the association. The association was short-lived, however, because when Moses returned, he destroyed the idol, disbanded the association, and chastised Aaron for his leadership among the people.

Ironically, yet another group emerged in response to the "golden calf association," namely the "sons of Levi," who volunteered to avenge the name of God. From this event one writer surmised the birth of the Levitical priesthood. Thus a permanent religious institution may have had its beginnings in relation to an informal voluntary association that was viewed by Moses and the writers of the Pentateuch as a negative historical connection.

Also in contrast to the "golden calf association" were those in the wilderness congregation of Israel who helped to create the Tabernacle. Individual voluntarism is laced throughout the narrative in Exodus 35 and 36. Moses reported God's command to take an offering from those "of a generous heart" (35:5). Later, after some associative consultation among themselves, without the benefit of any coercion from Moses, "everyone whose heart was stirred, and everyone whose spirit was willing . . . brought the LORD's offering . . ." (35:20-21), skilled workers, women and men. To reinforce the voluntary nature of the gifts, the writer recorded that it was "a freewill offering to the LORD" (v. 29). So great was the outpouring of the voluntary spirit that each morning additional freewill offerings were received until Moses had to restrain the giving, because what the people had already brought was more than enough to do all the work (36:6). One can easily see in this instance the inspiration for the later Christian experience of the voluntary parish altar guilds and sacristy associations that took special care of the sanctuary and the articles of a sacramental nature, as well as the example of abundant, spontaneous generosity.

The renewal of the Mosaic covenant at Shechem represents a significant expression of collective voluntarism among the Israelites. At the conclusion of Joshua's career, he gathered the tribes together to remind them of their covenantal responsibilities (Josh. 24:1-14). Joshua presented the crowd alternatives: "Choose you this day whom you will serve . . ." (24:15). In response the text reads, "we will serve the LORD, for he is our God" (24:18), and upon further interrogation by Joshua, "No, we will serve the LORD! . . . the LORD our God we will serve, and him we will obey . . ." (24:21, 24). While not a permanent association, this event demonstrates how easily voluntary associations formed in ancient Israel.

A more permanent associative example of religious voluntarism in the life of ancient Israel was the Nazarites. According to most scholars, Nazarites were a votive or prayer association of an unknown date of origin that apparently had both an involuntary relationship and a voluntary commitment.[1] Some who were classed as Nazarites obviously entered the order by virtue of a vow made by another, like a parent. This was the case with Samuel in 1 Samuel 1:11. Of the voluntary kind, some scholars see two traditions: those who voluntarily took the vow for a lifelong commitment and those who took the vow for a stated period of time. Whatever the period of commitment, Nazarites pledged themselves to an ascetic lifestyle that carried food prohibitions, a dress code, and prohibitions against contact with a corpse. Separation unto God was a high calling for the Nazarite association and carried with it the role and distinction of prophets and holy men. Samson, for instance, was a self-proclaimed Nazarite (Judg. 16:17). In the New Testament, it is thought by many that John the Baptizer was a Nazarite (Matt. 11:18), as was perhaps Saul of Tarsus (Acts 21:23).[2]

An example of task-oriented religious voluntarism may be found in the Palestinian Jews organized by Nehemiah during the Exile to rebuild the walls of Jerusalem. The fifth-century-B.C.E. narrative indicates a spontaneous reaction to Nehemiah's call to rebuild the city walls: "Come, let us rebuild the wall of Jerusalem, so that we may no longer suffer disgrace" (Neh. 2:17). The respondents included Jewish priests, nobles, officials, and workers, who "com-

---

1. Consult the article by J. C. Rylaarsdam, "Nazarite," in the *Interpreter's Dictionary of the Bible,* vol. 3 (New York: Abingdon Press, 1962), 526-27.

2. R. K. Harrison, "Nazarite," in *The International Standard Bible Encyclopedia,* vol. 3, ed. Geoffrey W. Bromiley et al. (Grand Rapids, Mich.: Eerdmans, 1986), 501-2.

mitted themselves to the common good" (2:18). There is no comment that the association received any compensation for their labour; rather, Nehemiah states that many refused the governor's food allowance and provided for their own necessities (6:14-18). Beyond the actual reconstruction effort, there was also the generosity of ancestral families toward special projects: gold, silver, priestly robes, and the like (7:70-73). Ultimately, the renewed Jewish community took a voluntary covenant to keep the law of Moses and to maintain the care of the Temple (10:28-39).

The term "sons of the prophets" may suggest a voluntary association around the prophets of ancient Israel. The discipling process among the prophets has early historical evidence, as in the case of Eli and Samuel. In 1 Samuel 3, "the boy Samuel was ministering to the LORD under Eli" (3:1). What follows is the story of the tenth-century-B.C.E. call of Samuel and his discipleship with Eli, which culminated in Samuel's recognition as "a trustworthy prophet of the LORD" (1 Sam. 3:19-20). Later, in the sixth century B.C.E., there is the relationship between Elijah and Elisha. In 1 Kings 19, it is recorded that Elijah passed by Elisha and threw his mantle over him. Elisha bade farewell to his family, "set out to follow Elijah and became his servant" (19:19-21). The eighth-century-B.C.E. prophet Isaiah called upon his disciples "to bind up the testimony and seal the teachings" among his followers. Isaiah's followers were "signs and portents" in Israel from the Lord of Hosts (Isa. 8:16-18). Baruch, the seventh-century-B.C.E. disciple of Jeremiah, was a spokesman (36:10), an emissary (36:18), a scribe (36:19), an organizer (43:3), and an oracle himself (ch. 45). It was apparently common for prophets to maintain a following of those who would voluntarily commit themselves to that mission in Israel.

The Old Testament narratives also contain numerous examples of personal voluntarism. Esther, for instance, exhibited great religious and ethnic heroism and acted upon her convictions by protecting her people at a critical moment. The judges also portrayed a kind of voluntarism that provided leadership for the nation in the thirteenth through the eleventh centuries B.C.E. One could also argue that the prophets exemplified a spontaneous, voluntaristic style in announcing their oracles to Israel. What emerges most clearly in the biographical sketches of many Israelite heroes is a pattern of faithfulness in response to God that served as a paradigm of spontaneous personal expression.

The Psalms may provide an insight into yet another illustration of voluntary behaviour, if not voluntary association, in the religious life of Israel. In both the tabernacle and temple periods of Israel's cultic development, individuals, groups, and the community at large were expected to worship and make sacrifices for various circumstances in their life experiences. These situations were of five kinds: payment of tithes, sickness and distress, special legal procedures, atonement for sin, and payment of special vows.[3] It is reasonable to assume that some of these activities were carried on in group associations as families or kindred were voluntarily faithful to their obligations. Passages that illustrate the requirements include Deuteronomy 26:1-11 (first fruits and tithes), Leviticus 14:1-32 (sickness), and Exodus 22:1-14 (restitution in unjust circumstances). As part of individual voluntary expression, a psalm of lament such as Psalm 109 might be used: "For wicked and deceitful mouths are opened against me, speaking against me with lying tongues" (109:2). A family of farmers might associate at the Temple and, with the assistance of a priest, recite words from Psalm 67: "The earth has yielded its increase; God, our God has blessed us" (v. 6). On a regular basis, Asaph and his family may have constituted a voluntary association of singers and musicians during the reign of King David (see 1 Chron. 16 and Ps. 105).

During the intertestamental period, voluntary associations became an important means of addressing various shades of religious and political affirmation of Jewish identity. As renegade Jews who sympathized with Hellenists urged people to cooperate with Antiochus IV Epiphanes, others resisted and associated to defend their faith and tradition. The general term to describe the loyalist element was "Hasidim," and of these a prominent group was the family of Mattathias, called Maccabeus. According to 1 Maccabees 2:42, the

---

3. A full discussion of these cultic practises and the use of the Psalms is found in John H. Hayes, *Understanding the Psalms* (Valley Forge, Pa.: Judson Press, 1976), 13-20.

Hasidim were "stalwart volunteers in the law." At first they hid in remote places; later Mattathias headed a revolt and swept through the countryside pulling down pagan altars and forcibly circumcising all the uncircumcised young boys. Following Mattathias' death, his son Judas led a second generation, "with the support of all his brothers and his father's followers, and they carried on the fight for Israel with zest" (1 Macc. 3:1). Here is a clear case of militaristic religious voluntarism in the third century B.C.É.

What one finds, then, in Israelite history and literature is a variety of premodern evidences of religious voluntarism. Some situations illustrate the encouragement of voluntary behaviour and performance thereof; others display a natural tendency to cooperate when a goal or task needs to be accomplished. Still other circumstances seem to suggest the beginnings of permanent associations of religious voluntarists that played an important role in the definition and life of a religious community.

II. The New Testament

It is in the Christian Scriptures that the voluntary principle in religious association took firm rootage. The teachings of Jesus of Nazareth, the organizing principle of the early Apostles, and the practises of the early churches all make a compelling case for a noncoercive form of religious experience and association. In the early Christian communities, practise preceded theological reflection. Thus important associations voluntarily coalesced and were fairly firm by the time of the first literary record in Scripture.

A. Jesus of Nazareth

Jesus of Nazareth may well have patterned his mission after the style of John the Baptizer. John is known to have created an apostolate (or following of committed disciples), doubtless based upon voluntary service. John's lifestyle was crude and simple and offered few rewards. Further, John called upon his hearers to voluntarily repent of their misdeeds. In this regard, John the Baptizer was not unlike other charismatic teachers and leaders, such as those associated with the Zealots or the Teacher of Righteousness in the Essene community during the Roman period of Jewish history.

The canonical Gospels record that when Jesus created his circle of followers, he did so by invitation. Typically he "called," that is, invited, people to follow him. In hindsight, Christian interpreters have underscored the authority of Jesus to bring people to his cause as though in a predetermined fashion. The dynamics of Scripture, however, paint a different picture. The reader learns, for instance, that the word *akoloutheo*, translated "follow," conveys the meaning "coming after, accompanying, going along with,"[4] seeming to signify a willing commitment. Not only did individuals become Jesus' disciples voluntarily, but large crowds followed him voluntarily (Matt. 4:25). During his trial, some even followed voluntarily at a safe distance (Mark 14:54)!

The basic ethic of Jesus' ministry was predicated upon a voluntaristic response and voluntary service. Here are the roots of a theology of voluntarism. Discipleship was an act of one's own choosing. The cost of discipleship was a voluntary commitment: "If any want to become my followers, let them deny themselves and take up their cross daily and follow me" (Luke 9:23). Self-denial and cross bearing thus became important ideals in the New Testament community, which sought to imitate Christ as closely as possible. Peter recalled simply that Jesus "went about doing good" (Acts 10:38). The rewards for such commitment were not obvious in material terms or self-interest, so Jesus reminded his new followers in his Sermon on the Mount to avoid preoccupation with material pursuits. Rather, they were to expect that their reward for voluntary service for God would be the provision of life's essentials. To the seventy evangelists he advised, "Carry no purse, no bag, no sandals . . . remain in the same house eating and drinking whatever they provide, for the laborer deserves to be cared for" (Luke 10:4).

4. William F. Arndt and F. Wilbur Gingrich, *A Greek-English Lexicon of the New Testament and Other Early Christian Literature* (Cambridge: University Press, 1957), 30.

Jesus laid out a voluntary basis for his disciples' association in Luke 12:32ff. He first asserted the voluntary benevolence of his Father's purposes: "your Father has chosen gladly to give you the kingdom" (v. 32). This divine attitude is to be an example and motivation for disciples to live free of material concerns: "seeking the kingdom first . . ." (v. 31). In order for disciples to be dependant upon God's provisions, they are instructed to sell their possessions and give to charity, in other words, to translate their assets into love gifts. Here would be a foundation for voluntary Christian service and benevolence in the later history of the church. This and similar passages clearly teach an attitude of self-giving over self-preservation and profitability.

In his encouragement to prayer, Jesus again taught a voluntary principle: "Ask . . . seek . . . knock . . ." (Matt. 7:7) — all verb forms associated with personal initiative. Seeming to reflect God's own initiative, disciples are given the opportunity to approach their heavenly Father in expressing their needs, desires, and aspirations. In God's omniscience, God already understands the questions and has the resources, but wishes to be approached voluntarily by human beings. Much is revealed about God's personal character and human similarity in Jesus' instructions to prayer.

Jesus' words to the woman of Samaria in John 4:21-24 reveal a voluntary character to his understanding of worship. Those who would worship God must do so "in spirit and truth": the term *aletheia*, translated "truth," conveys the moral value of integrity, uprightness, and sincerity. In the context of the Father's "seeking" (*zetei*), a voluntary response in worship is the only acceptable attitude. Rather than a command to worship God, as the Israelite or Samaritan law would have provided, the basis of worship in the new spiritual economy is to be demonstrably voluntary.

One of the fondest depictions of Christ in the Gospels and the Apocalypse is that of the "inviting Christ." In Matthew 11:25ff., Jesus issues a warm invitation to all those who would voluntarily accept his instruction, identification with his mission, and comfort. The message is repeated in Revelation 3:20, "Behold, I stand at the door and knock . . . if anyone hears and opens. . . ." Acceptance of the principles of Christ was an altogether voluntary matter.

The ultimate illustration of the voluntary principle in the life of Christ was his voluntary submission to the will of his Father that he should die. Jesus was incarnated in human form and enjoyed full control over his choices, and he exercised that freedom. In John 10:17-18, he made the ultimate voluntary decision and demonstrated his authority to do so:

> For this reason the Father loves me, because I lay down my life in order to take it up again. No one takes it from me, but I lay it down of my own accord. I have power to lay it down, and I have power to take it up again. I have received this command from my Father.[5]

To this can be added the interpretation of the Apostle Paul in Philippians 2:6-8, where he also used a reflexive pronoun to describe the voluntary sacrifice of Jesus:

> who, though he was in the form of God, did not regard equality with God as something to be exploited, but emptied himself, taking the form of a slave, being born in human likeness. And being found in human form, he humbled himself and became obedient to the point of death — even death on a cross.

B. The Apostolic Church

The disciples of Jesus followed his example of voluntary religious experience. The association took informal but identifiable shape after the Resurrection as a cluster of followers who enjoyed the common experience of Christ's earthly ministry. They were first a memorial association in the "room upstairs." Their purpose was to grieve over the loss of their leader and to recall with fondness their experiences with him. Later, after his appearances to them before his ascension, they would have in common the experience of the Risen Lord, most vividly perhaps his conversation with Thomas in which they wit-

---

5. The use of the reflexive pronoun here reinforces Jesus' point: "No one takes it from me . . . I lay it down from me. . . ."

17

nessed the reality of his Resurrection body. This pattern of a small apostolate would form the shape of the earliest assemblies described in the Book of Acts.

The historian of Pentecost asserted that the object of the apostles' ongoing informal association was to receive enablement for the task of evangelization. Drawing again upon the associative example of John the Baptizer, Jesus had informed his followers, "wait for the promise of the Father . . . you will be baptized with the Holy Spirit not many days from now" (Acts 1:4, 5). This "memorial association" met frequently and set about more formal plans of association. They first defined the membership criteria of their association: that select group who had been together with Jesus between his baptism by John and his ascension. Following the death of Judas, they elected a final member, Matthias, to fill out the number twelve. Membership qualifications were strictly maintained, as illustrated later in the case of Saul of Tarsus, who, it was reported, "attempted to join the disciples . . . [but] they did not believe that he was a disciple" (Acts 9:26).

It was on the day of Pentecost, as expected, that empowerment came when the apostles were baptized with the Holy Spirit and the "apostolic association" became official and formal. Soon after the signs and wonders of Pentecost, however, the objects of the association shifted in both number and substance: empowerment for evangelization became apostolic teaching, fellowship, breaking of bread, and prayers (Acts 2:42).

Water baptism, rich in the symbolism of the Spirit, became the initiatory rite of the association that characterized itself as an *ecclesia* ("church"), or gathering of those called out of the larger culture by the Spirit. Biblical theologians point out the importance of baptism as a public witness, a sign of personal identification with the risen Christ, and an expected common experience for the community. Baptism, it would appear, had a solidifying impact on the association and was practised throughout the churches of the first century. Of particular relevance in this matter was the role of baptism in the gospel traditions, where the first-century recorders of the words of Jesus were careful to demonstrate Jesus' own design for a voluntary association of persons baptized "in the name of the Father and of the Son and of the Holy Spirit" (Matt. 28:19).

The intimate relationships of the apostles and friends, plus the carefully guarded rite of baptism, thus provided the early Christian community with a high level of social identification and exclusiveness. To be a member of the Christian association was to profess a relationship voluntarily with the risen Christ, to support the life of the association voluntarily with gifts, and to absorb whatever social stigma and penalties might be forthcoming due to membership. The model of formal voluntary association that emerged in Jerusalem would become a premier paradigm for the Christian community.

As the movement spread throughout Jerusalem and Judea, and later far beyond Palestine, the apostles followed a voluntary pattern in other ways, such as in the support of the community and in the decision-making processes. In this regard, they emulated the association they had been a part of with Jesus of Nazareth. In Acts 2, a voluntary communalism emerged to meet the needs of the growing association: "All who believed were together and had all things in common; they would sell their possessions and goods and distribute the proceeds to all, as any had need" (v. 44). The historian noted the "glad and generous hearts" and "goodwill of all the people," signifying full assent to this arrangement. Beyond this radical economic voluntarism was the spread of communalism throughout the Jerusalem associations: Barnabas, a Cyprian Levite, sold real estate and presented it as a contribution to the apostles (Acts 4:32-37). Finally, when a severe famine was reported in the region during the reign of Claudius (A.D. 41-54), the voluntary spirit erupted among the broader Christian community and collections were received according to capability in order to meet the obvious humanitarian need.

The missionary work of the Apostle Paul presents an interesting set of circumstances for the historian in search of evidences of early Christian voluntarism. It is obvious that, in several cases, Paul visited and worked among established churches, while in others he appears to have worked and corresponded with less permanent associations. In Antioch, Corinth, and Ephesus, for instance, he related to churches, while in Philippi and Thessalonica he related to associations of people. In Thessalonica certain members of the Jewish synagogue "were persuaded and joined Paul and Silas, as did a great many of the devout Greeks and not a few of the leading women" (Acts 17:4). In a fascinating account of Paul's visit to Philippi, Luke records that "On the sabbath day we went outside the gate by the river, where we supposed there was a place of prayer; and we sat down and spoke to the women who had gathered there" (Acts 16:13). Whether this type of association reflects an entirely new organizational paradigm, as some suppose,[6] or one encounters rich examples of Christian voluntarism, the evidence is compelling for voluntary associationalism in the life of Paul.

The support of the ministry in Pauline tradition reflected a voluntary pattern also. Although Paul recognized the words of Jesus on the matter of compensation for preaching the gospel — "the Lord commanded that those who proclaim the gospel should get their living by the gospel" (1 Cor. 9:14) — he disclaimed compensation for himself so that others would not hold him accountable. He reminded the Thessalonians that "he worked night and day so that we might not burden any of you" (2 Thess. 3:8). In fact, Paul used a peculiarly complex voluntaristic argument to the Corinthian church in favour of voluntary service, namely, that if he preached the gospel of his own accord, as a profession, he should expect a reward. But as he saw it, he was under a commission of God to preach the gospel and thus could "make the gospel free of charge," not claiming his own rights (9:18). Paul had no desire to have his apostleship or the gospel of grace associated with the recognized cultic practises of the Temple, where the priests received a legally sanctioned but publicly criticized share of what was sacrificed on the altar. This ideal of voluntary ministry in the church has long been practised by lay-dominant and primitive-imitative forms of church life.

Decision making was of a democratic sort in the apostolic associations and reflected a latent voluntarism. When housekeeping duties threatened to diminish the role of apostolic leadership, a debate over forms of leadership was held and the diaconal ministry was born. This proposal "pleased the whole community," and the association took part in their rite of consecration (Acts 6:1-7). There was also debate in the Jerusalem associations over the matter of

6. Ralph D. Winter, "The Two Structures of God's Redemptive Mission," *Missiology: An International Review* (1974): 122-23, builds a case for the origins of "sodalities."

circumcision (Acts 11:1-18; 15:1-21) that was resolved "with the consent of the whole church" (Acts 15:22). This principle of democratic decision making was fundamental to the vitality of the spread of the Christian movement.

Beyond the evidences of voluntary organization in the New Testament are numerous references to voluntary associations of a social or religious kind in the classical tradition. In ancient Greece, citizens formed religious associations devoted to mystery cults and philosophical schools. Similarly, in Roman society, various sorts of clubs called "collegia" were formed among every class of society. For those involved in business and commerce, clubs provided civic and personal services. At times of celebration, these associations heralded the emperor or honoured important events and persons. Another group of Roman voluntary associations were involved with religious purposes; collecting around a particular deity, members formed a cult and enjoyed regular camaraderie. Still others in the lower classes could be members of burial societies or other social groups that took care of important functions of personal and group welfare. Several scholars have pointed to the similarity, if not dependance, of the early Christian communities on these secular models as vehicles of early Christian voluntarism.[7]

III. Summary

What may be deduced, then, from both the Judeo-Christian Scriptures and intertestamental Judaism is a picture of cultural activities central to which was a voluntary impulse. Historians of Israel recorded voluntary coalitions of people for various purposes, and heroic figures illustrate the importance of spontaneous action. In the

---

7. On the development of the models in Greece and Rome, consult Samuel Dill, *Roman Society: From Nero to Marcus Aurelius* (New York: Meridian Books, 1956) and the articles on "clubs" in *The Oxford Classical Dictionary*, ed. M. Carey et al. (Oxford: Clarendon Press, 1949). The possible connections with the Christian tradition are discussed in John E. Stambaugh and David L. Balch, *The New Testament in Its Social Environment* (Philadelphia: Westminster Press, 1986), 124-26.

Christian tradition, some of the voluntarism was spontaneous and modelled upon secular social experience; a deliberate quality of voluntarism, with a modest theological basis, emerged in the first generation of Christian experience.

While the writers of the canonical New Testament (particularly Saul of Tarsus) were careful to ascribe to God the appropriate qualities of sovereign grace and a perfect will, they repeatedly underscored the importance of human response. Such voluntarism is illustrated in Jesus' definitions of discipleship, his offers of salvation, and his own example of self-sacrifice. In the early church the nature of service, care for the community, and support of the ministry were all of a voluntary style, as was the process of making decisions in the early Christian congregations. It is not overstating the case to assert that the apostolic churches were a carefully created network of voluntary associations.

CHAPTER TWO

The Theological Bases of Christian Voluntarism

The principles of voluntarism begin in the Christian understanding of God. God is affirmed in Christian creeds as Creator, Sustainer, Redeemer, and Judge. It is in God's nature as Creator that the idea of "voluntariness" begins. Early Christian thinkers blended several theological ideas and metaphors, which left Christian thought with a distinctly voluntary ethos.

In general, voluntary theology begins with a description of God's nature, to the extent that God's nature can be described. In the biblical revelations, God is depicted as acting both out of self-interest and for the benefit of creation. In God's own interest, God created human beings for God's pleasure and companionship. God acted out of the freedom of God's own will and opportunity. God had at least two choices: to create that which guaranteed God's pleasure and satisfaction by ensuring its choices, or creating that which possessed alternatives. God chose the latter, reflecting God's own nature, and set in motion a series of seemingly endless acts of human volition. Thus part of the "creation mandate" was that God's people should engage in responsible and charitable works, among their other pursuits of subduing the earth.[1]

---

1. I am indebted to Professor C. H. Pinnock of McMaster Divinity College for this useful phraseology. While early modern voluntarist theologians stressed this principle, it was recovered in later evangelical and holiness theologies.

One approach to comprehending human experience in Christian theology has been to articulate in doctrinal formulations human behaviour as the result of the human will. Behaviour was understood to be a continuous activation of what is in humanity's best interests: pleasure, absence of pain, fulfillment, meaning, and enrichment. Ethical decisions are thus fundamentally made on this basis. Classical theologians early referred to this decision-making capability — specifically "volition" — as part of the *imago dei*. Humans determine through the use of reason, act through the will, and receive whatever consequences ensue. Orthodox theologians have always reminded the Church that God is the source of all of these "graces," but "popular" theology ascribed at least the results to observable human circumstances and relationships, in some ways presaging the debate between theology and modern behavioural sciences.

If, then, humans have "usable" capabilities, how may these be applied to God's purposes in the world? If God is at work in humans individually and socially, much attention must be given to how humans go about exercising freedom of the will and how and to what end human benevolence is channelled. The prior question Christian theologians dealt with was whether humans have a free will and are capable of acceptable benevolent acts. A more specific survey of selected classic theologians will illustrate the evolution of voluntarist theology.

I. Voluntarism in the Church Fathers

A. Origen: An Optimistic Theologian

Origen (185-253), the principal teacher of the catechetical school of Alexandria, was a primary catalyst in the development of voluntarist theology. In particular, Origen's concept of the incarnation of Christ led to a view of human capability that was dramatically optimistic.[2] One of the most creative of the Church Fathers, Origen was distinctly influ-

---

2. W. H. C. Frend, *The Rise of Christianity* (Philadelphia: Fortress Press, 1984), 377-78.

enced by the Greek philosopher Epictetus (c. 50–c. 130), who taught that the gods had given humans the abilities of choice and refusal.

Beginning with a Platonic separation between God and creation, Origen argued that Christ was the necessary and logical link between the two and that the divine and human natures of Christ illustrated how humans have the capability to act towards God. Next, he used a Platonic construct to classify created beings on the basis of movement: some things moved when acted upon, like stones, while other things had the capacity in and of themselves to move. Rational beings have the capability through reason to make choices and move of their own will. Humans have this ability and are responsible for their decisions and actions. He thus vitiated the positions of both the Gnostics and the Marcionites, and helped to establish a strong and full Christology and a strong doctrine of humanity.[3]

For Origen, Christ enabled humans to progress towards ultimate fulfillment. Freed from the doctrines of heaven or hell, education became for Origen the realization of God's intention for humanity. Of the temptation to exercise free will harmfully, Origen argued that discipline would prevent this. In his own experience, he observed "how frequently unruly people were made chaste and savages became gentle."[4] At the end of his famous dialogue with Heracleides, Origen exclaimed, "Let us take up that which depends on our own decision. God does not give it to us. He sets it before us. 'Behold I have set life before thy face.'" Origen clearly had in mind a race of enlightened Christians without distinction of race or class, as W. H. C. Frend observed.[5] Origen's high view of human capability and freedom of choice was well in keeping with the intellectual attainments of Alexandria, then considered the intellectual capital of the Mediterranean world. More was not made of Origen's position, however, because later theologians emphasized his teaching of the pre-existence of the human soul and universal restoration, both of which were condemned by Pope Virgilius in A.D. 554.

3. John W. Trigg, *Origen: The Bible and Philosophy in the Third Century Church* (Atlanta: John Knox Press, 1983), 116.
4. Trigg, 117.
5. Frend, 380-83.

B. Pelagianism: A Lost Tradition

The theology of Augustine of Hippo (354-430), with its particular emphases upon the depravity of humanity and original sin, came to dominate Latin, or Western, thought. This dominance overshadowed a debate in the fourth century that had much to do with human volition and voluntarism. In fact, Augustine's descriptions of Pelagius have prejudiced all modern assessments of the issues.[6]

Augustine built his case on the sovereignty of God that included a strong assertion of the providence of God, by which Augustine meant God's rule over history so that God's will is accomplished. Once human free will was activated in history, God works through human agency and events, not against or in spite of them. Human sinfulness has frustrated God's gracious designs and human will is so bound in sin, thought Augustine, that only by the gracious providence of God is humankind redeemed. God respects human free will, neither willing nor creating the evil that characterizes human history. As other historical theologians have observed, for Augustine the voluntary exercise of human free will, before or after salvation, was largely negative and destructive.[7]

Another approach was advanced by Pelagius, a contemporary of Augustine. Pelagius was a teacher from Britain who went to Rome about A.D. 400. There he was startled by the immorality in the city and began to emphasize humans' responsibility for their actions in his teaching and writing. His focus upon free will seemed to Augustine and later teachers of Catholic doctrine to exclude the importance of the grace of God, and thus he was ultimately condemned at the Council of Carthage in A.D. 418.

But on second look, Pelagius was a prime mover in the development of voluntarist thought and certainly laid the ground for later

6. For an assessment of the impact of Augustine's theological position in the Western church, see Clyde L. Manschreck, *A History of Christianity in the World* (Englewood Cliffs, N.J.: Prentice Hall, 1985), 67-79. There is a resurgence of interest in the question of the freedom of the will. See David Basinger, *The Case for Freewill Theism: A Philosophical Assessment* (Downers Grove, Ill.: InterVarsity Press, 1996).

7. On this point, see Langdon Gilkey, *Reaping the Whirlwind: A Christian Interpretation of History* (New York: The Seabury Press, 1976), 160-68.

theories of human capability and freedom. His thinking deserves attention here.

Pelagius's entire system, if it may be called that, was predicated upon three premises: (1) that Adam neither injured his descendants nor deprived them of anything; (2) that there are no sinful people, only wrongful acts of the will; and (3) that a person is free if one does what one wills and avoids what one wishes to avoid. Pelagius thus argued that there is no inherent incapacity to humans, that in fact they can "will" and "do" according to their opportunities.[8]

Pelagius further believed that God gave to each person the ability (*posse*) to will (*velle*) and to act (*esse*) in freedom. Each person is held accountable for his/her acts. Christ, therefore, issued commands, clearly implying human capability and freedom to respond in obedience. Pelagius used the Matthean passage "But you must always act like your Father who is in heaven" (5:48) to illustrate his point. Righteousness, he asserted, is the opposite of sin and the desired goal of the human will. In fact, the entire New Testament is filled with injunctions that are built on the premise that humans are expected to respond and possess the capability to do so.

The followers of Pelagius carried forth his ideas of enlightened human capability. Celestius, for instance, asserted that the representative nature of Adam for the sins of the human race and of Christ as the representative of all humanity in the Resurrection was not valid; rather, each person sinned or was perfect in his/her own right and would be raised individually in the Resurrection. Julian of Eclanum, another student, followed the Nicene Creed on the doctrine of baptism, but went further, as his teacher Pelagius had suggested, in stating that infants should be baptized not because of their inherited sin from Adam, but because baptism would make them better and renew them as children of God. Unfortunately for the orthodox dimensions of Pelagianism, the tradition was moved from the mainstream by an overpowering Augustinian bias.[9]

8. Manschreck, 73.

9. The "Augustinian triumph" does not explain the ongoing character of British Christianity to exhibit traits of nonconformity and voluntarism. A recent examination of Celtic Christianity, for instance, argued that voluntarism was a

II. Developing a Theology for Collective Benevolence

The second question in the evolution of voluntarist theology that posed a challenge for the Christian Church was to determine the validity of collective Christian benevolence. If individuals were capable of exercising their freedom to do good works, could individuals in association with others achieve a collective good?

For centuries, benevolent works had been defined and administered by the Church through the bishops and holy orders. Penitential acts to remit sins and corporal acts of mercy generated a regime of good works of both spiritual and physical kinds.[10] Gradually as the *via moderna* called forth the limitless possibilities of collective human creativity in other political and economic pursuits, like the development of cities and trade, Christian administrators and thinkers were pressed to revise their guidelines on collective Christian endeavour. Moreover, the increasing complexity of western Christian society after the eleventh century posed greater needs to which the gospel might be applied, such as aiding victims of a plague or evangelizing northern Europe. For the twelfth-century Christian, new opportunities for the individual led naturally to dynamic forms of possible collective service: missions, benevolence, and humanitarian involvement. Beguines (sisterhoods), beghards (lay brotherhoods), and other tertiary orders of laypersons voluntarily engaged in care for the sick and poor and preaching supplemental to the clergy.[11] The eminent contemporary theologian Thomas Aquinas

---

central feature of that tradition in contrast with Roman conformity. See Caroline M. Stellings, "The Earliest Dissenters: The History and Historiography of the Celtic Church" (unpublished M.T.S. thesis, McMaster University, 1995), 105-6.

10. Swanson, *Religion and Devotion . . .* , 206, 218-20. On the corporal acts of mercy, consult J. M. Perrin, "Acts of Mercy," in *New Catholic Encyclopedia,* vol. 9 (New York: McGraw Hill, 1967), 677. The corporal acts were derived from Matthew 25:34-40 and 1 Corinthians 3:16, and include: feed the hungry, give drink to the thirsty, clothe the naked, harbor the stranger, visit the sick, minister to prisoners, and bury the dead, seven acts in all.

11. The beguine movement is believed to have arisen in part as a response to the abundance of single women and widows (*frauenfrage*) in the thirteenth and fourteenth centuries. The accompanying men's movement, particularly popular in

(1226-1274) provided a theological rationale for such effort by defining *charity* as "the mother of all virtues" because "it initiates the action of other virtues by charging them with life."[12] Doing good had a penitential dimension for individuals as well as fulfilling the mandate of the medieval Church to provide collective care for society. Overall, the Church hierarchy maintained close scrutiny over these examples of spontaneous voluntarism because some had the potential for heterodox directions.[13]

A. Francis and Christian Benevolence

One of the great examples of this newly found collective Christian activism that catalyzed change was Francis of Assisi (1181-1226). Francis was an Italian Christian enthusiast whose preaching attracted a significant following of persons who desired to emulate Francis's simple lifestyle and engage in his works of personal benevolence. In 1210 he wrote his first rule, and in 1217 the Order of Franciscans (Friars Minor) was started, with papal recognition in 1223.

Several elements of Francis's teaching bear directly upon a theology of Christian voluntarism. First was his affirmation of lay ministry. The vast majority of Francis's early followers were drawn from laypersons like builders, merchants, and members of guilds. Rather than form a brotherhood of the clergy, Francis sought people who would work for their livings at the trades they previously practised. When the living was insufficient, the brothers were to beg. Early records of the first order indicate that, for their worship needs, the Franciscans depended upon masses in local congregations by ordained priests.

Belgium, was drawn from the lower classes of fullers, weavers, and dyers. The vows of both groups were voluntary and not irrevocable. See Ernest W. McDonnell, *The Beguines and Beghards in Medieval Culture; With Special Emphasis on the Belgian Scene* (New Brunswick, N.J.: Rutgers University Press, 1954), 81-100, 129, 246-65.

12. Thomas Aquinas, *Summa Theologica,* vol. 34 (London: Blackfriars, 1964), 32-33.

13. The Free Spirit heresy of the thirteenth century and the Waldensians of the fourteenth century exemplify this possibility.

Second, Francis reinforced the notion of a deep personal commitment to Christian service. According to his disciple Bonaventure (1221-1274), Francis derived his theological understanding from experience and this paved the way for new voluntaristic emphases.[14] Francis's own simple lifestyle and sacrifice drew many to his call: he took literally Matthew 10:7-10. One's initial commitment to work with Francis was thus entirely voluntary. The early accounts of Franciscan discipleship are abundantly clear that the converts had great enthusiasm to join the movement and later to take the vows and live by the rule. At the heart of the Franciscan ideal was obedience to the gospel: each aspirant had to sell all that he had and distribute his goods to the poor as prescribed in Matthew's Gospel.[15]

Francis introduced new forms of Christian service that met explicit needs of his social context. Many congregations in Italy had languished, and the first effort was evangelism, with the brothers going out in clusters of two. Their basic strategy was preaching, and the preaching style apparently was convictional and called forth respondents. In addition, the followers of Francis engaged in food and clothing distribution for the poor. In several towns, church buildings were restored. Francis visited and worked in leper colonies and, beginning in 1212, gave assistance and encouragement to the building of hospitals.[16]

While little case can be made for the Order of Franciscans as a voluntary movement after vows were taken, important patterns of benevolence were laid. Building practically upon Augustinian and Anselmian constructs, Francis believed in the value of individual and collective good works as part of the charitable and penitential demands of Christianity. His selection of works from evangelism to

14. Jaroslav Pelikan, *The Growth of Medieval Theology (600-1300)* (Chicago: University of Chicago Press, 1978), 305-6. Little is known directly of the sources of Francis's theology, and he left no systematic articulation.

15. John Moorman, *A History of the Franciscan Order from Its Origins to the Year 1517* (Oxford: Clarendon Press, 1968), 8-19.

16. Moorman, 24; Lazaro Iriarte, *Franciscan History: The Three Orders of St. Francis of Assisi* (Chicago: Franciscan Herald Press, 1983), 130-31, lists the poorhouses, hospitals, leper houses, and work among widows, orphans, and others that the Franciscans began and turned over to the territorials.

humanitarian efforts set in motion new lay energies in the Church, as well as suggesting a renewed institutional role for the Church. Francis's and his followers' early interest in missionary efforts to the Holy Land, northern and central Europe, England, and Africa portrays a new direction in the expansion of Christianity, not by the power of conquering papal legions but by the persuasion of preaching and humanitarian service. These would be important patterns for later voluntarists.

III. Erasmus: The Will Recovered

Among those seeking reform in the Church, the debate over human effort continued. John Duns Scotus (c. 1265–c. 1308) and William of Occam (c. 1280–c. 1349) each contributed new perspectives on the issue. Duns proposed that humans of necessity will their own good and that the power of choice is a primary human attribute. In a related philosophic direction, William of Occam advocated for Christian believers acts of charity or morally benevolent acts. It was this type of anthropological transformation in the late Middle Ages that provided an intellectual cradle for modern theological emphases, of which voluntarism would be an important component.

In the Renaissance, it was Desiderius Erasmus (1466-1536), a Dutch scholar, writer, and editor, who rejoined the issue of the freedom of the will. A sometime lecturer at Oxford, in his many-faceted career he advocated toleration and an enlightened view of humanity. Adding to his stature as a Christian theologian, Erasmus became embroiled in a protracted debate with Martin Luther in 1518 over the question of the freedom of the human will. That debate revealed much of where the mainstream of Western Christianity was practically headed.

In his Heidelberg Catechism of 1518, Luther maintained that free will after the Fall was corrupted. In a tract two years later, he described good works as "damnable sins" if done to gain credit with God. Erasmus responded in a tract called *Concerning the Freedom of the Will* (1524) and later in *Hyperaspistes* (1527). The crux of Erasmus's position was that, while humans cannot be perfect and salvation is by faith alone, the theory of a completely corrupted human will does not do justice to all of Scripture. What did one make of the passages that promised a reward for faithful works and those many injunctions that implied that humans had the capability to respond to God? Erasmus held that God enables humans to do good and that humans cooperate with God in working out their own salvation.[17] In a sharply worded rejoinder to Martin Luther, Erasmus asserted that God is a tyrant if God condemns humans for what they cannot help. Thus, humans must have some control over their actions. For Erasmus, God was like a loving parent who enabled a child to take his/her first steps under his/her own power. Therefore, not only did humans exercise free will as a gift of God's grace, but Christians were expected to perform works as God's people in the world.[18]

In the world of the Renaissance, Erasmus's theology reflected emerging realities. Following the lead of Francesco Petrarch (1304-1374) and Giovanni Pico della Mirandola (1463-1493), philosophers and scientific theorists recognized that nature and human society were more interesting and compelling than sacramental theology and the pursuit of immortality. "Man" and his potential became the central feature of creation. Bold philosophers/theologians cautiously followed suit: Della Mirandola allegorized in his *Oration on the Dignity of Man* (1485) that the greatest gift of God to human beings was "genius": ". . . with freedom of choice and honour thou mayest fashion thyself in whatever shape thou shalt prefer."[19] Artists expressed themselves on canvas in painting individuals; architects blended the classical tradition with the gothic style in the design of

17. Jaroslav Pelikan, *Reformation of Church and Dogma (1300-1700)* (Chicago: University of Chicago Press, 1984), 138-41.

18. Roland H. Bainton, *Erasmus of Christendom* (New York: Charles Scribner's Sons, 1969), 188-89.

19. Pico della Mirandola, *Oration on the Dignity of Man,* 224-26. On the relevance of Pico, compare J. M. Rigg, ed., *Giovanni Pico Della Mirandola: His Life by His Nephew Giovanni Francesco Pico, translated from the Latin by Sir Thomas More* (London: David Nutt, 1890), with William G. Craven, *Giovanni Pico Della Mirandola, Symbol of His Age: Modern Interpretations of a Renaissance Philosopher* (Geneve: Librairie Droz, 1981), esp. 77-89.

church and secular buildings; and scholars laboured successfully to collect or translate the long-lost literary classics of the ancient world. Little wonder, then, that Erasmus could not accept Luther's refusal to dignify in any respect human free will and capability. The movement to which the term "humanism" was applied, and of which Erasmus was an exponent, well exhibited the new discovery of human potential and accomplishment. While reformers like Luther and Calvin, for instance, held tenaciously to Augustinian assessments of humanity, Erasmus signalled the real future of practical theology.

IV. Baptists and a Voluntary Theology of the Church

A small group of English Nonconformists at the beginning of the seventeenth century actually devised a theology of the Church that was comprehensively voluntaristic. Under the leadership of John Smyth (fl. 1605) of Gainsborough and later Amsterdam, a congregation of believers arrived at an understanding of community and Christian experience that was a true break with precedents. Here was a concept of voluntarism that was not extraneous to the purpose of the Church, but at its very definition.

Smyth and his followers found much fault with the Church of England for its unreformed practises and ideas of membership. Puritans for a time, and for a few years among the ranks of Separatists, the fledgling congregation continued to study the Scriptures. At last in 1608, Smyth and his friends agreed to a voluntary covenant "to walk in all God's ways made known or to be made known to them." Next they constituted a church of true believers, who voluntarily professed their faith and voluntarily submitted to a new believer's baptism. They were convinced that no other form of the church was valid, largely because in some form or another, coercion was present.

The Baptist movement in England took several directions, each expressing some form of voluntarism. General Baptists emphasized that Christ died for all persons, freed by the redemption of Christ to respond to the gospel. Particular Baptists were more cautious about the action of humans in God's sovereign plan of redemption, but insisted upon a voluntary commitment to the church and

33

believer's baptism. In their earliest expressions of a common theological understanding, the Particular Baptists stressed that they were "joined to the Lord by mutual consent."[20] Thirty years later they again stressed the voluntary nature of their churches: "The members of these Churches . . . do willingly consent to walk together . . . giving up themselves to the Lord and to one another. . . ."[21] This voluntary principle of organization extended to relationships between congregations and with other worthwhile groups of Christians.

The Baptist movement, which extended early in its history to the American colonies, carried a completely voluntary theological doctrine of the church. The corollaries to this basic premise were an antagonism to interference from governments and churchly authorities that led to the principle of the separation of church and state, an emphasis upon the value of an individual believer that led to a doctrine of complete religious liberty, and a loose confederation of cooperating churches for the sake of a task like missions or education. Other nonconformist sects would follow the lead of the Baptists; indeed, their ecclesiology would become a dominant motif in American and Canadian voluntarism (see Chapter Four).

V. John Locke: Voluntarism Finally Defined

Following more than a century of bitter debate and civil wars in England, a new enlightened era began with the Act of Toleration in 1689. The towering figure of this early stage of the English Enlightenment was John Locke (1632-1704).[22] A medical doctor who had lived

20. *The Confession of Faith of Those Churches That are Commonly (though falsely) Called Anabaptists* (London, 1644), Art. 33.

21. *Confession of Faith Put Forth by the Elders and Brethren of Many Congregations of Christians (Baptized upon Profession of Their Faith) in London and the Country* (London, 1677), 26:6.

22. An important assessment of the political and social context of the English Enlightenment and the expansion of the bourgeoisie is found in Robert Wuthnow, *Communities of Discourse: Ideology and Social Structure in the Reformation, the Enlightenment, and European Socialism* (Cambridge, Mass.: Harvard University Press, 1989), 169-79.

in both England and the Netherlands and was a keen observer of church life in social contexts as well as a student of theology, Locke was among the first to define sharply the nature of the voluntary church and its theological foundation. Locke's best arguments for toleration — or a voluntary Christianity — were the nature of a religious community and the inevitable limitation of human knowledge. Based upon observations of society in Holland, Locke developed a sophisticated understanding of social institutions, out of which he viewed England as an interconnected series of "societies" — some for business, trade, intellectual, and religious purposes. Locke spoke of the commonwealth as a society of persons constituted only for preserving and advancing their civil goods — their central design was to protect their property.[23] Conversely, he thought the purpose of religious societies to be the care of souls and pursuit of eternal life. Since these two tasks involved inward persuasion of God's Spirit, an earthly magistrate had no right or authority to coerce human conscience. The political principle that he espoused was that church and state are "separate societies," into each of which persons enter voluntarily and for distinct purposes.

An enlightened view of freedom and human capability undergirded Locke's concept of toleration. "He is free who can do what he wills to do," Locke believed; opportunity was as important as the old arguments over volition.[24] Toleration, therefore, was absolutely essential to allow individuals to choose freely and to maintain which religious society they desired, or none at all. Reason, not force or law, was the best promoter of true religion. Intolerance, on the other hand, was unjustifiable because no church or human possessed the full truth. In addition, intolerance was ineffective; the true weapons of a church should be example and persuasion. "All the life and power of true religion," he wrote, "consists in the inward and full persuasion of the mind."[25]

23. C. B. Macpherson, *The Political Theory of Possessive Individualism: Hobbes to Locke* (London: Oxford University Press, 1964), 197.

24. Joseph J. Rickaby, *Freewill and Four English Philosophers: Hobbes, Locke, Hume, and Mill* (Freeport, N.Y.: Books for Library Press, 1969), 107.

25. Locke, *Works* . . . , VI, 10; Richard I. Aaron, *John Locke* (Oxford: Clarendon Press, 1971), 293ff.

John Locke was well immersed in the Nonconformist theology of the church as a voluntary society. In his famous *Letter on Toleration* (1689) he wrote:

> Let us now consider what a church is. A church seems to me to be a free society of men, joining together of their own accord for the public worship of God in such manner as they believe will be acceptable to the Deity for the salvation of their souls.
>
> I say it is a *free and voluntary society.* Nobody is born a member of any church . . . no man is bound by nature to any church or assigned to any sect, but he voluntarily joins the society in which he believes he has found true religion . . . if he discovers anything either erroneous in the doctrine or incongruous in the worship, he must always have the same liberty to go out as he had to enter.[26]

In so defining the church, Locke reflected fourscore years of evolution of church/state theory and the advances of Dissent legalized in the Act of Toleration.[27]

But Locke's thought moved a step further concerning the internal nature of the church. A church is also entitled to have its laws, he theorized, to prescribe membership qualifications, conduct its affairs in an orderly way, and manage its business. Importantly, however, there is no set pattern of doctrine or structure that Christ empowered by edict; thus authority cannot be claimed for any single system. Each person must decide what is legitimate; and, it is taken for granted, there will be a variety of opinions that necessarily allows a freedom of choice. Locke was well aware of the variety of structures and styles; his toleration extended to "Remonstrants, Anti-Remonstrants, Lutherans, Anabaptists and Socinians, even to Pagans,

26. *The Works of John Locke: A New Edition, Corrected,* vol. 6 (London: Thomas Tegg, 1823), 13.

27. For a comprehensive treatment of this subject, see W. K. Jordan, *The Development of Religious Toleration in England, From the Convention of the Long Parliament to the Restoration 1640-1660* (Gloucester: Peter Smith, 1965), 538-42, especially his comment that "the Baptists clung to the principle of absolute freedom with amazing and heroic consistency."

Mahometans, and Jews." In a free society, any group that presented a reasonable case for itself and operated according to social propriety was worthy of allegiance and financial support.[28] Thus Locke signalled to Christians, as well as social and political theorists, the maturation of a new form of church life and structure completely voluntary in participation and support.

Given John Locke's influence in the eighteenth century upon social contract and political theories, his views on toleration, undergirded by his definition of *all* churches as voluntary societies, are of major import for the evolution of religious voluntarism in the West.[29] Not only did his views win widespread acceptance in the wake of the Act of Toleration in Great Britain; he became the favourite of the French Enlightenment thinkers as well.[30] Moreover, it was a generation of later politicians and church leaders in the United States and British North America who put Locke's theories to the test where toleration and voluntarism became the prevailing tendency.[31]

VI. Practical Theologians in the Voluntary Tradition

A. The Pietists

Following the several branches of the Protestant Reformation, most of the newly formed bodies settled down to a theologically defined "confessional Christianity." Observers then and historians since have noted the relatively stale condition of the churches in the German

---

28. *Works of John Locke,* 37, 47, 52, 55.

29. William G. McLoughlin, *New England Dissent, 1630-1833: The Baptists and the Separation of Church and State* (Cambridge, Mass.: Harvard University Press, 1971), I, 519-20, 600-601, shows how dependant major thinkers in the American colonies such as Isaac Backus were upon John Locke's definition of a church for both legal and constitutional reasons.

30. John W. Yolton, *Locke and French Materialism* (Oxford: Clarendon Press, 1991).

31. Thomas L. Pangle, *The Spirit of Modern Republicanism: Moral Vision of the American Founders and the Philosophy of John Locke* (Chicago: University of Chicago Press, 1988), 117-27.

states, Switzerland, and Scandinavia. In part a reaction to this circumstance and in part a spontaneous eruption of spirituality, a
widespread movement called "Pietism" emerged in England, central
Europe, and eventually in the American colonies. Pietism was characterized by a devotion to Scripture, a personal experience with
Christ, renewed worship, a commitment to mission, and social action. The movement lasted from the end of the sixteenth century to
the early eighteenth century; included in its prominent proponents
were Johann Arndt (1555-1621), Philipp Jacob Spener (1635-1705),
August H. Francke (1663-1727), and Nikolaus Ludwig, Count von
Zinzendorf (1700-1760). Traces of the Pietist tradition may be seen
in modern evangelicalism.

Pietist thinkers were not original in that much of what they
propounded was based upon the earlier confessions. They often
rationalized their ideas directly from the confession or by a reference
to Scripture. Of their need to stress good works, Lutheran Pietists
maintained that they were merely being faithful to the twentieth
article of the Augsburg Confession of 1530 and the Heidelberg
Catechism of 1518.[32] Against charges of subjectivism, the theology
of the confessions was a sure defence.

In contrast with scholastic theology, Pietist thought began with
the supposition that theology is a practical discipline that consists
of more than study and knowledge: exercises in practical Christianity
and edification are equally relevant. For Spener, the ethic of love
undergirds all practical works. Basing his views on passages like John
13 and 1 John 3, he understood that the Lord commanded his
children to love one another and then express general love toward
all people (2 Peter 1:7).[33] Johann Arndt taught that the practise of
such love would lead to seeking every opportunity to render one's
neighbour a service.[34] Ultimately, this impulse led Pietists to organize

32. So argued the most distinguished historian of the movement: F. Ernest
Stoeffler, *The Rise of Evangelical Pietism* (Leiden: E. J. Brill, 1971), 10-11.

33. Philipp Jacob Spener, *Pia Desideria*, trans. Theodore G. Tappert
(Philadelphia: Fortress Press, 1964), 87-122.

34. Quoted in *Pietists: Selected Writings*, ed. Peter Erb (New York: Paulist
Press, 1983), 37.

associations and institutions to assist in education, children's work, care for foreigners in a given city, orphanages, and training in the trades.[35] Pietists liked to feel that such work was done in obedience to Christ and reasoned that it was a testimony to their salvation. Their efforts represent an early modern form of voluntarism.

B. The Puritans

Generally speaking, the Puritans of England and early America would not be considered exemplars of Christian voluntarism. As perhaps the most consistent Calvinists of their era, they had as a central feature of Puritan experience an all-embracing determinism. This prevented much speculation about how the works of God's people might be transformed into a major ethical urgency. In addition, American Puritans, practising a communal ideal, held to a doctrine of mutual subjection as a "sinew of society." This had the net effect of reducing individual human effort to a minimum. Puritans placed their main emphasis on vocation, that is, every person was to locate God's place and work of blessing and pursue it with zeal.[36]

What did emerge in Puritan circles was a modest encouragement to engage in charitable works. Puritans understood society to be inherently unequal, and this was due to the greater blessing of God upon some people than upon others. The result, practically speaking, was that some had the means to assist others, within certain limits. Puritans in England first held that the Poor Laws needed to be enforced. The truly needy were to be an opportunity for the elect to exercise their faithfulness. Governor John Winthrop of Massachusetts (1588-1649), in his tract *A Modell of Christian Charitie*

---

35. A typical list is found in "Outline of All the Institutes at Glauch near Halle Which Provide Special Blessings Partially for the Education of Youth and Partially for the Maintenance of the Poor as the Institutes Exist in December 1698," in Erb, ed., 163-64.

36. William Haller, *The Rise of Puritanism* (Philadelphia: University of Pennsylvania Press, 1972), 83; Allen Carden, *Puritan Christianity in America: Religion and Life in Seventeenth-Century Massachusetts* (Grand Rapids, Mich.: Baker Books, 1990), 135.

(1630), urged the high motive that the poor of the community had a right to expect charity from the rich because God had given the means to the rich to "perfect the bond of brotherhood."[37] The result was a personal voluntary mixture of prayer, almsgiving, and care for the sick. The eminent Cotton Mather (1662-1727) offered an extensive listing of projects and needs worthy of Christian attention.[38] Ultimately this type of charity seems to have benefited the benefactor more than the needy, as it increased the status of the donor in the eyes of his/her peers.

In English Puritan history, one major outpouring of Puritan voluntarism possessed great possibilities. When news of the discovery of native Americans in the Puritan geography of New England reached England, Puritan divines immediately accepted responsibility for the conversion of the Indians as a God-given task. In 1651 Parliament was persuaded to incorporate what became the New England Company; this provided not only a legal foundation to Indian charity but also a compelling ecclesiastical reason to give to the mission in New England. John Eliot (1604-1690), the leader of the Puritan effort among the Indians, thought that the best reason for giving was in response for what God had done in prospering the community of faith:

> Come forth, ye Masters of Money, part with your Gold to promote the Gospel; Let the gift of God in temporal things make way for the Indians' receipt of spirituals . . . if you give anything into banke, Christ will keep account thereof and reward it. . . . And as far as the Gospel is mediately advanced by your money, be sure you will be remembered.[39]

The evangelization of Indian peoples fit neatly into the Puritan concept of Christian responsibility, as it emphasized God's provi-

37. John Winthrop, "A Modell of Christian Charitie," in *Massachusetts Historical Collections,* vol. 7 (Boston, Mass.: Massachusetts Historical Society, 1864), 31-48.

38. Cotton Mather, *Bonifacius: An Essay on the Good* (Boston, Mass.: B. Gretz, 1710). See also Carden, 135-36.

39. *The Glorious Progress of the Gospel Amongst the Indians in New England* by J. D., a Minister of the Gospel (London: Edward Winslow, 1649), 27.

dence in placing the Indians at the instance of the English; it emphasized the translation of the Scriptures; and it challenged the zeal of Protestants against the advances of the Jesuits.[40]

C. Anglican Voluntarist Thought

The theology of Anglican voluntarism in the late seventeenth century also occupies a significant role in the developing tradition of collective Christian experience. Anglicans moved to establish voluntary societies and to martial the significant resources of their population to support their works of charity. It was not so much a creation by a single person, but the collective understanding of wealth and property and Christian responsibility to do works of charity that comprised the Anglican tradition. Leaders like Thomas Bray (1656-1730), Robert Nelson (1656-1715), Henry Ashurst (1614-1680), and a host of cooperative bishops were primary voices in making the case for Christian voluntarism.

At the root of Anglican thought was a conviction not unlike that expressed by the Puritans a half century earlier:

> This principle is as manifest as the very being of God Himself:
> . . . He hath provided all things necessary for their subsistence. . . .
> And yet, by the dispensations of Providence the good things of
> this life appear to be scattered with so unequal a hand, that there
> are thousands upon earth that possess nothing; from whence it
> will follow, that either Providence hath been wanting to Mankind
> in necessaries; or that the portion of the Poor is lodged in the
> hands of the Rich; either GOD hath neglected the Care of those
> who are destitute of every thing, or He hath devolved that Province
> upon those who possess all things in Abundance.[41]

The case, then, began with the assumption that there is an inequity in the material world that Christians could voluntarily alleviate. The

---

40. William Kellaway, *The New England Company 1649-1776* (London: Longmans, Green & Co., 1961), 21.

41. "Some Reflections Upon the Foregoing Address," 224-25.

next step was to identify classes of people who could respond to different theological appeals, like the merchant class and those of significant means. The merchants had a Christian responsibility to act through their gifts as a work of recompense for those who had added to their well-being. Those who were wealthy were to give to enhance their Christian experience. As the "Pious" Robert Nelson commented, "why should not those who have a design upon Heaven, and carry their views into Eternity, be as wise for the Good of their souls?"[42]

Anglican bishops were especially fond of the argument from English Christian culture. It became for them a sacred duty of the English nation to Christianize those benighted peoples of the world and to give them the gifts of English culture. The Bishop of Lichfield and Coventry in 1705 commented, "Not only the Honour of our Nation and the figure it makes in the World but the strength and security of it depends upon a well-established Trade. . . . And how would this advance if our people abroad were brought under a sober Sense of Religion . . . ?"[43] The material reality of the investment in colonial charity was ever present to the Bishop of Sarum, when he extolled the charitable possibilities of his city: "It is the glory of this city and a glory beyond the magnificence of its buildings or the vastness of its trade that it is the greatest Fund of charities now in the world. . . ."[44]

An eschatological dimension was added to some of the theological appeals. Gifts in the earthly life would lead to rewards in the life to come, thought several writers. Charity was one of the best courses to manifest thankfulness to God, "from whom they hope to secure no less than eternall happiness and glory."[45] A similar line of

---

42. Robert Nelson, *An Address to Persons of Quality and Estate* (London: G. James, 1715), 103.

43. *A Sermon Preached at St. Mary-le-Bow, February 16 1704/05 Before the Society Incorporated for That Purpose Exhorting All Persons in Their Stations to Assist So Glorious a Design* (London: Downing, 1705), 24.

44. Lord Bishop of Sarum, *A Sermon Preached at St. Mary le Bow, February 18 1703/04 Before the Society Incorporated for That Purpose Exhorting All Persons in Their Stations to Assist So Glorious a Design* (London: Jos. Downing, 1704), 23.

45. *An Abstract of the Charter Granted to the Society for the Propagation of the Gospel in Foreign Parts; With a Short Account of What Hath Been and What Is Designed to Be Done by It* (London: n.p., 1703), 3.

argument developed in support of legacies for the Anglican societies after 1715 as it became obvious that the annual subscription campaigns were producing insufficient funds in the first decade of the Society for the Propagation of the Gospel (founded 1701). The last act of voluntary expression that a faithful person of means could accomplish was a gift to ensure the work of a society.

Often the cogency of the theological assertions of Anglican leaders was powerfully assisted by the identity of key leaders of the church. It was, therefore, an important example of voluntarism to have bishops, the archbishop, and the sovereign express their support for Anglican projects and to present a gift of their own.

D. John Wesley

John Wesley (1703-1791) was doubtless the most popular theological English-language writer of his century. A teacher, evangelist, church administrator, and theologian, he made important contributions to the theology of voluntarism. Wesley was indebted theologically to the Pietist writers and William Law (1686-1761), and philosophically to John Locke, whose writings he pursued for an intellectually respectable faith and whose views on religious societies Wesley enjoyed himself.[46] In his upbringing can be found evidences of Puritan and Anglican thought and experience in a case for Christian voluntarism; his father started a society for local moral reformation, and Wesley was well read in Puritan works.

Wesley was driven by a zeal for good works, a phrase that occurs often in his sermons and journal and that he borrowed from the New Testament Epistle to Titus (3:8). When, for instance, he was confronted by Joseph Butler, Bishop of Bristol, for preaching without permission in Bristol, Wesley replied, "My Lord, my business on Earth is to do what good I can. Wherever therefore I think I can do the most good, there must I stay so long as I think so."[47]

---

46. Richard E. Brantley, *Locke, Wesley, and the Method of English Romanticism* (Gainesville, Fla.: University of Florida Press, 1984), 8-13, 28-32.

47. This conversation is detailed in Frank Baker, "John Wesley and Bishop

For Wesley, good works acceptable to God were made possible by the cooperation of God and human faithfulness. Wesley was quite sensitive to charges that he was a Pelagian (i.e., that he supported a doctrine of works righteousness), and he asserted that "it is God that not only infuses every good desire, but that accompanies and follows it. . . ." Once a person has tasted salvation, the steps Wesley suggested were to flee from all sin, carefully avoid evil conversation, and be zealous of good works, the latter meaning works of mercy and works of charity.[48]

Works of mercy and works of charity covered a wide expanse for John Wesley. He held that it pleases God for believers not only to engage in works of devotion like the study of Scripture and prayer, but also as means of grace to perform deeds of mercy. In his sermon on "visiting the sick," Wesley saw a range of spiritual rewards for the visitor, such as patience, meekness, gentleness, and longsuffering; he also saw it as a duty of those who are in good health and have the time and resources to apply to the public good. Here was a revisitation of the argument of the earlier Anglicans like Anthony Horneck (1641-1697), who felt that those who are fortunate have a responsibility for those less fortunate. Wesley went even further to state it as an obligation: those who desire to inherit the Kingdom of God would consider it an obligation to visit the sick.[49]

From his childhood, Wesley clearly supported Christian endeavour through voluntary associations. He was active in the Reformation of Manners movement and frequently spoke to annual meetings of societies. As he grew older, he developed his own theological rationale for voluntarism in works of charity. In a famous sermon preached before the Humane Society in 1777, he argued that a criterion of God's judgement upon believers would be their faithfulness in good works. On God's authority, and using the biblical metaphor of a tree that bears much fruit, Christians are to feed the

---

Butler: A Fragment of John Wesley's Manuscript Journal, 16th to 24th August 1739," *Proceedings of the Wesley Historical Society* 42 (May 1980): 93-100.

48. "On Working Out Our Own Salvation," in *The Works of John Wesley*, vol. 3, ed. Albert C. Outler (Nashville: Abingdon Press, 1986), 203.

49. "On Visiting the Sick," Outler, ed., 385-93.

hungry, give drink to the thirsty, assist the stranger, and clothe the naked. Wesley extolled the virtues of associations like the Humane Society and urged its work upon his followers.[50]

As an evidence of their salvation, Wesley wrote that Methodists were to "do good of every possible sort, as they had opportunity and as far as possible to all persons." In his "Rules for the United Societies" (1743), his followers were enjoined to be volunteers in a number of pursuits, starting with their fellow members of the Christian community. Associations for commerce, preferential treatment in employment, assistance in business, and spiritual accountability were all legitimated in the rules. As well, Methodists were to involve themselves in associations that worked among the sick, imprisoned, homeless, and heathen. In a teaching closely akin to the Anabaptist doctrine of suffering, Wesley advised his followers that self-denial, voluntary cross bearing, and absorbing the reproach of Christ would receive their ultimate reward.[51] History elsewhere has shown the leading role that Methodists played in exercising social concern both through their own associations and by support of other benevolent institutions.

E. William Carey and Popular Voluntarism

Mention should be made in the context of Baptist contributions to a theological understanding of religious voluntarism of William Carey (1761-1834). Although he was removed by over a century from the origins of Baptist voluntarism in the evolution of Baptist ecclesiology and theories of religious liberty, Carey represents a next logical step in the development of Baptist and, by extension, Christian voluntarism.

The context for Carey's thought was evangelical Calvinism, particularly as it was articulated in preacher-writers like Andrew

---

50. "The Reward of Righteousness," Outler, ed., 403.
51. "The Nature, Design, and General Rules of the United Societies in London, Bristol, Kingswood, Newcastle-Upon-Tyne, etc.," in *John and Charles Wesley: Selected Writings and Hymns,* ed. Frank Whaling (London: SPCK, 1981), 108-10.

Fuller (1754-1815), a Baptist pastor in Kettering, England. Fuller argued to the satisfaction of a growing number of pastors and prominent laypeople that Christians have an obligation to preach the gospel. The persuasive power of preachers to bring people to conviction was the paramount objective of ministry for Fuller, and it presupposed an enlightened view of human voluntarism.[52] His good friend William Carey built upon the sense of ministerial obligation and created a compelling case for the obligation of all Christians to use means to convert the heathen.

Carey recognized the importance of theoretical and practical religious liberty. Not only were all persons entitled to a free choice in religious matters, but it was also evident that religious liberty was being practically extended in his generation. The importance of the growth of religious liberty was that it presented a greater opportunity for unbelieving people to respond to the gospel. Carey had no problem extending the enlightenment views of human capability, well established in Britain in the eighteenth century, to all the peoples of the earth. He even went so far as to catalogue their whereabouts.[53] The universal attribution of human capability to respond to the gospel was his first great contribution to a Baptist theology of voluntarism.

For William Carey, the voluntary principle had an equally important second dimension. Not content merely to pray fervently for the conversion of the heathen, Carey proposed the use of "means" to conduct evangelization effectively. Here he unashamedly created a theological rationale from the commercial sector by arguing that in the same way that a trading company extends its interests to maximize its profits, so also Christians must use every means to extend their work of evangelization. Carey was well aware of the efforts of earlier Catholic, Anglican, Pietist, and Lutheran organizations and their circumscribed limitations. What he called for was a fully cooperative, multiconfessional voluntary society of persons "whose hearts are in the

52. Andrew Fuller, *The Gospel Worthy of All Acceptation; Or the Obligations of Men Fully to Credit Whatever Means God Makes Known, etc.* (Northampton: T. Dicey, 1785), 146.

53. William Carey, *An Enquiry into the Obligation of Christians to Use Means for the Conversion of the Heathen* (Leicester: Ann Ireland, 1792), 38-66.

work, men of serious religion and possessing a spirit of persever-
ance. . . ." "There is room enough for us all," he continued, "without
interfering with each other. . . ."[54] In short, Carey believed that voluntarist enthusiasm could override sectarian jealousies.

William Carey's third contribution to Christian voluntarism was
in the development of a vehicle for popular participation. He asserted
with full acceptance the Anglican theology of stewardship of the
wealthy, namely that those who were blessed with much success have
a responsibility to support evangelization. But Carey went further, to
claim the participation of persons of all socioeconomic classes. From
the Puritans he borrowed the idea that a tenth of one's annual increase
should be devoted to the Lord's work. Further, he urged congregations
to set aside a penny per week toward a missions fund, and finally he
observed that those who boycotted West Indian sugar because of the
slave trade had saved their families between six pence and a shilling
per week that could be given to missions.[55] In short, Carey believed,
every Christian individual could share in Christian voluntarism as an
act of faithfulness to Christ. In William Carey a Baptist theology of
voluntarism would thus reach its fullest expression.

F. Robert A. Fyfe

The contributions of Robert A. Fyfe to practical voluntary theology
are not as well known as others, but significant nonetheless. Fyfe
(1816-1878) was a Canadian Baptist educator and theologian who
helped to define voluntarism in the particular context of nineteenth-
century British North America. His theological ideas reflect classical
Baptist thought on the one hand and the additional evolution of
nineteenth-century individualism on the other.

Fyfe's voluntarist theology began with his view of the church,
as his biographer pointed out.[56] He wrote of a church, "It is a

54. Carey, 83-84.
55. Carey, 86.
56. Theo T. Gibson, *Robert Alexander Fyfe: His Contemporaries and His Influence* (Burlington, Ont.: Welch Publishing Co., 1988), 122.

company of immersed believers, who from a sense of duty from their Saviour, have voluntarily united themselves together for the purpose of more carefully carrying into practise the doctrines and precepts of the gospel."[57] He emphasized the nature of membership as predicated upon a voluntary confession of faith, a voluntary baptism, and a voluntary submission to the requirements of membership.

Second, Fyfe held that the church was to be composed of "real believers," saints, people with a particular calling. This means that their allegiance is ultimately to the gospel and the Lord of the church. The typical believer has an obligation to support what he/she believes in and without compulsion from the state or an ecclesiastical hierarchy. Likewise, independent congregations should support voluntarily organizations for mission and educational purposes, as in the New Testament examples. Much akin to John Smyth, the General Baptist pioneer of the early seventeenth century, Fyfe held that only the support of God's people should undergird benevolent projects; there should be no public or governmental support for the church or its institutions. Christian believers have a sacred responsibility from God to provide the support; and if they did not or could not, Fyfe thought the institutions were not worthy of continuation.

Fyfe held that Christ's church was stronger and better endowed than any human institution, and this emanated from the power of Christ to use the church as his instrument to perform God's gracious design. Fyfe knew from his own experience that God had placed it in the heart of certain Christians to be generous and to build the voluntary support needed by benevolent institutions. His position became the theological and practical foundation for the establishment of a "voluntary" pattern of support for church-related institutions in Upper Canada and was materially useful in creating a uniquely Canadian usage of the term "voluntarism."[58]

57. *Montreal Register*, 28 March 1844.
58. Many of Fyfe's theological ideas are excerpted from J. E. Wells, *Life and Labours of Rev. R. A. Fyfe, D.D.* (Toronto: W. J. Gage, 1885), 145ff.

Summary

Beginning with the first-century Christian writers, notably Saul of Tarsus, the issue of human capability was debated widely. Ever at stake in the discussions were the necessary doctrines of God's sovereignty and human sinfulness. Some writers, notably Origen and Pelagius, experimented with stressing human free will. Due to Augustinian reaction, this tendency was relegated to heterodoxy. Later, a more practical theology emerged as Christian leaders like Francis of Assisi responded to a call to do good works. Still later, under the influence of what came to be known as the European Renaissance, fear and distrust of human freedom gave way to an enlightened Christianity; Christians like the Baptists and individuals like John Locke built for a future of toleration and freedom. The theological debate, for all practical purposes, ended with the Enlightenment and was succeeded with attempts to develop a practical theological basis for Christian voluntarism. In this regard, Pietists, Puritans, Anglicans, and Methodist theologians made important contributions. What came next was the application of the newfound willpower in associations and societies that would proliferate on both sides of the Atlantic.

CHAPTER THREE

Modern Historical Antecedents

While church scholars, working largely in the medieval tradition, continued to debate Augustinian/Pelagian positions, church organizational evolution called forth new opportunities and new energies. The modern voluntary impulse was, in a very real sense, a gift of the Protestant Reformations. The dissolution of a universal church, even into continuing state churches, illustrated a broadly based recognition that more than one approach to being the church and conducting Christian mission and benevolence was valid. New leaders, new institutions, and new processes soon followed.

The expansion of European Christendom into the Far East and the western hemisphere activated the impulse toward voluntarist Christianity. In addition to the traditional orders of Roman Catholic evangelization, members of the Jesuit order organized in 1663 a Society of Foreign Missions that sent missionary priests to China and the Americas. In North America, Catholics vied with the Church of England, the Reformed tradition, Presbyterians, Lutherans, and a host of unruly English sectarians. In so-called Latin America, the battle was between several forms of Catholicism: Spanish, Portuguese, French, and the various religious orders in competition with each other. This well-told frontier pluralism changed forever the strategies of Old World Christendom.

I. English Christianity Leads the Way

English Christianity during the Tudor period enjoyed its last phase of Erastian thrust. Commonly, it was the bishops who determined where new parishes would be erected and what benevolent projects warranted approval. It was Parliament that determined the tone of public morality and acceptable liturgy. This traditional style of managing Christian life and endeavour was best illustrated in the strategies the Crown used to administer Christianity in newly claimed colonial possessions. The monarchy assumed the authority to claim lands and resources for "God and King," and authorized the territorial rights of the established church in the early charters of Newfoundland, Virginia, and New England.[1]

With the Puritan Revolution, however, much changed about the conduct of Christian mission and who should be involved. First, the Puritan government was convinced it had a responsibility to conduct Christian mission. An important geographical prospect was New England, and the specific target was the aboriginal population. Leading Puritans like John Eliot, Edward Winslow (1595-1655), and Henry Ashurst all believed it was incumbent upon the Christian Commonwealth to use all practical means to civilize and convert the Indians. Their concern was threefold: to obey the gospel, to rescue the "savages" from the yoke of Spanish Catholicism, and to assert Protestant Christian responsibility in the New World. The first two worthy goals contrasted with the imperialism of the third objective in a Parliamentary bill passed in July 1649, entitled "An Act for the Promoting and Propagating the Gospel of Jesus Christ in New En-

---

1. John R. H. Moorman, *A History of the Church in England* (London: Adam and Charles Black, 1953), 221-29. The documentation of colonial establishment is found in Edwin S. Gaustad, ed., *A Documentary History of Religion in America*, vol. I (Grand Rapids, Mich.: Eerdmans, 1982), 97ff.; good assessments of the struggle for a colonial American voluntary way are found in Winthrop S. Hudson, *Religion in America: An Historical Account of the Development of American Religious Life* (New York: Scribner's, 1973), 32-58; Sydney E. Ahlstrom, *A Religious History of the American People* (New Haven: Yale University Press, 1972), 99-117; and John F. Woolverton, *Colonial Anglicanism in North America* (Detroit: Wayne State University Press, 1984).

gland." This legislation established a corporation or society that could conduct legal business to achieve the evangelization of the American Indians. The "New England Company" thus became the oldest English Protestant missionary society.[2]

The New England Company was the fountainhead of the voluntary system in English Christianity; it was also the commencement of churchly voluntarism. Composed of sixteen persons who were predominantly successful merchants of London and involved in one way or another in the colonial enterprise, the Company essentially collected money to spend on approved projects, which included printing of John Eliot's tracts, support for schools, and publication of related literature. Money was received in several ways: gifts, estates, collections, and real estate transactions. What made the New England Company a voluntary association was its organizational structure and its primary financial resource. As an organization, it had members and officers who were unpaid and were involved on a casual basis. There was a certain social and religious prestige, to be sure, in belonging to the Society; however, no one was compensated. The primary source of funds was the response of persons in local parishes and the well-to-do who gave in response to the announced appeals.

The New England Company was transformed at the Restoration in 1661 into a chartered royal corporation that was quite distinct from its predecessor. What had been a Puritan circle of state-sponsored Christian endeavour became a Nonconformist company composed of Presbyterians, Independents, and Baptists. Once it was reorganized with a larger board, salaried employees were hired to handle the projects and manage the accounts, annuities, and real estate. The members of the corporation still served gratis, but the primary outreach to parishes and wealthy individuals was changed forever.[3]

Based squarely upon the experience of the New England Company was the vision of Thomas Bray. Bray spent the early part of his

---

2. So begins its latest official history, William Kellaway, *The New England Company 1649-1776: Missionary Society to the American Indians* (London: Longmans, Green, 1961), 1.

3. Kellaway, 166ff.

career in parishes and chaplaincies across England. He had observed the Religious Society movement under the leadership of Anthony Horneck, which emphasized spiritual formation, as well as the Societies for the Reformation of Manners, in which prominent voluntarists like Edward Stephens (d. 1706) participated.[4] In key points of ministry, Bray built a number of well-placed friendships that would later assist him in his ventures. In 1695, Bray had the good fortune of being selected by Bishop of London Henry Compton (1632-1713) to assess the condition of the Church of England in Maryland and Virginia colonies; this led to his proposal for a mission to improve the quality of ministry as well as religious education in general. In the late 1690s, with Bishop Compton's support, Bray devised a plan whereby the English colonies in America would be the beneficiaries of a Christian library system under the auspices of the Church of England; he also proposed a new system of catechetical schools and libraries in England itself, to be organized by the Church. Recognizing the novelty of his ideas, plus the existing claims on Church finances and personnel, Bray suggested establishing a "Congregation Pro Propaganda Fide," or voluntary association of eminent lay gentlemen, to provide the resources and management of gifts, legacies, and grants for these projects. Bray's initial concept actually became two distinct organizations: the Society for Promoting Christian Knowledge (S.P.C.K.), formed in 1698, and the Society for the Propagation of the Gospel in Foreign Parts (1701). Following the firm establishment of his initial two associations, Bray ventured farther into voluntary pursuits, creating, for instance, in the 1720s "Bray's Associates" for founding clerical libraries and Negro schools.

The S.P.C.K. was a purely voluntary association dedicated to providing useful Christian literature for a literate public, supporting publication of the Scriptures, establishing schools, and promoting

---

4. On the Religious Society movement, see Josiah Woodward, *An Account of the Rise and Progress of the Religious Societies in the City of London, etc. and of their Endeavours for the Reformation of Manners* (London: n.p., 1712), and specifically on the Manners groups, consult the contemporary *An Account of the Progress of the Reformation of Manners* (London: n.p., 1704) and the recent study of Dudley W. R. Bahlman, *The Moral Revolution of 1688* (New York: Archon, 1968).

the faith of the Church of England. Those first generations of Society members included prominent clergy, such as the Bishop of London and other bishops of prominent cities, plus poets, businessmen, lawyers, teachers, and politicians.[5]

Bray's vision, however, required more than he could accomplish in the S.P.C.K. This led to the second organization, the Society for the Propagation of the Gospel in Foreign Parts (S.P.G.), formally chartered three years later. Like the New England Company of fifty years before, the S.P.G. had official legal status to receive bequests, transact legal affairs, and engage in real estate transactions. Its stated objects were to care for the religious needs of American colonists by maintaining the sacramental ministry of the Church of England and to work for the conversion of the heathen — which came to mean aboriginal peoples, Roman Catholics, and occasionally Puritans. The membership of the Corporation was specified and included the archbishop, several bishops, knights, gentry, and king's chaplains. The charter guaranteed that the S.P.G. was the official organ of the church to conduct missionary purposes; and, from the early records, the leaders of the Society were the officers of the church. The official historians of the S.P.G. believed that its closest parallels were the chartered trading companies, which facilitated overseas commerce with the East Indies, the American Colonies, and Russia.[6] It wasn't long before the members of the predominantly Nonconformist New England Company were protesting the interference of the S.P.G., given the latter's far-ranging interests in the northeastern colonies.

In what way were these Anglican organizations voluntary? Although church leadership, bishops, and diocesan processes governed the personnel and staff work of the S.P.C.K. and the S.P.G., the basic income was derived from contributions, called "subscriptions," and

5. The best-documented study of the S.P.C.K. is W. O. B. Allen and Edmund McClure, *Two Hundred Years: The History of the Society for Promoting Christian Knowledge 1698-1898* (New York: Burt Franklin, repr. 1970), 13-122.

6. The most modern account of S.P.G. is H. P. Thompson, *Into All Lands: The History of the Society for the Propagation of the Gospel in Foreign Parts 1701-1950* (London: S.P.C.K., 1950).

given voluntarily.[7] The theory was that the wealthier the "member," the greater the subscription. To enhance the subscriptions, the needs of the S.P.G. were put before the public in some extraordinary ways. The annual meetings of the society were a public spectacle, with the pomp and circumstance of church and royal officialdom in attendance. Public attention to the mission enterprise was thus achieved. The royal family infrequently was persuaded to announce a formal appeal, which drew the interest of the upper classes. The published subscription lists always made much of the examples of prominent Christian donors, in the hopes that the example would be heeded by those of the church in general. One could also argue in the Anglican tradition that in their roles as members and officers of the societies, the leadership was unpaid and not acting as an official department of the church. Well into the history of the S.P.C.K. and the S.P.G., Anglican historians described these venerable associations as voluntary.[8]

Unhappily, by the conclusion of the eighteenth century, voluntary support for both the S.P.C.K. and the S.P.G. languished; the older society had difficulty supporting its overseas work in India, and the total voluntary receipts of the S.P.G. amounted to under one thousand pounds per year in 1798. Moreover, the rising tide of Anglican lay interest — styled "evangelical" and tied to the larger revival — was disenfranchised from the older two societies, whom the evangelicals classed as "high church." Men like Thomas Scott (1747-1821), John Venn (1759-1813), and Richard Cecil (1748-1810) believed they were led to become involved in mission and were anxious to organize a new Anglican association. According to what they called the "church principle," which harkened back to the primitive New Testament church, sixteen clergy and nine laymen began in April 1799 the Church Missionary Society (C.M.S.).

The primary support for this third Anglican mission society was again the individual contribution. Contributions within the first few

7. H. P. Thompson, *Into All Lands: The History of the Society for the Propagation of the Gospel in Foreign Parts 1701-1750* (London: S.P.C.K., 1951), 16; Allen and McClure, 25.

8. Eugene Stock, *The History of the Church Missionary Society: Its Environment, Its Men and Its Work,* vol. 1 (London: Church Missionary Society, 1899), 65.

years amounted to almost five hundred pounds annually, with the larger contributions being fifty to one hundred pounds each. At length, as the industrious founders retired from voluntary service, the C.M.S. secretaryship became a salaried position, but the management and policy-making functions remained in the hands of a voluntary board.

The foundation of voluntary support for missions was thus laid in the British culture by renewal in the Church of England. It was a pattern not lost on Nonconformists. With the passage of the Act of Toleration (1689), new means opened for numerous associations, hitherto discouraged from collective Christian work.

Among the first Nonconformists to organize voluntary associations for a variety of religious purposes were the Presbyterians. In their transition from a state church to a denomination, the Presbyterians built a network of cooperative ventures to assist their denominational interests. In London in July 1690, thirteen ministers, mostly Presbyterians with a few Congregationalists, formed an association to provide for voluntary preaching and the support of young persons for the ministry. Calling themselves the "Presbyterian Fund," they concentrated their disbursements on England and Wales; by 1720 this "Fund" had evolved into a domestic missionary society.

Ever suspicious of Presbyterian designs, English Congregationalists separated from the 1690 venture after five years and formed their own "Congregational Fund." Typically, the Congregational Fund was much more egalitarian in management style than the Presbyterians; ultimate authority was vested in messengers of the congregations. This first voluntary venture for a specific task beyond the local church signalled the beginnings of a new denominational reality for English Congregationalists.

Baptists also moved into a new era of organization as a result of the Act of Toleration. From the earliest expressions of the Baptist congregations to cooperate with each other and with other Independents and Presbyterians, Baptists pursued a well-defined course of voluntarism. As the first churches were gathered, offerings were described as "freewill" and limited to members only; support was not allowed from those who were not part of the covenant. Great stress was placed upon lay involvement and ministry of all the congregation (see Chapter Two). Churches in the London area in the

1640s voluntarily met together to form nonbinding associations, and an important pattern was cut.

Following Toleration, Baptists ventured into other areas of cooperation that required creativity and new forms of extra-parish organization. In the 1690s, the matter of ministerial education was widely discussed, leading eventually to "funds" being established in both major branches of the denomination. These funds were cooperative associations of clergy who received gifts and distributed monies according to need. Similarly, Baptist clergy in London formed in 1714 a "ministerium" to link with other dissenting denominations to address matters of mutual concern like legal property rights, estates, and ordination status. Education proved to be the area of greatest voluntary cooperation among British Baptists before William Carey envisioned the application of the voluntary principle to missions.

Recognizing the Crown's continued attempts to control dissent, several major groups organized a collective body to address common realities. This was the Three Dissenting Denominations, later known as the Dissenting Deputies. The unpopular Test Act of 1702 probably was the catalyst for cooperation among the Presbyterians, Particular Baptists, and Congregationalists. All of these groups desired recognition of their rights to hold property, to register marriages and such, and to receive bequests. Also, it became useful to maintain a master list of clergy, to which all of the urban congregations contributed. Eventually, the Dissenting Denominations put forward a programme of political unity to address the issues of concern to Nonconformists in Parliament. Within the next century, the Dissenting Deputies were a major coalition in the English political process.

By the 1770s, the stage was thus set for the momentous events of the 1790s that insured the future of English-speaking evangelicalism would be voluntarist.

II. The Launching of a New Era

Many religious historians now make a definite connection between the eighteenth-century religious awakenings and the rise of religious voluntarism. Two important roots may be identified in this regard:

the Great Awakenings in North America and the Wesleyan Revival in Britain.

In both instances, spiritual forces were unleashed among large numbers of common people. In the colonies, the mass meetings of George Whitefield (1714-1770) attracted hundreds from Massachusetts to Georgia to his sermons of evangelism and discipleship. Whitefield's preaching led to the establishment of orphanages, academies, and pro-revival churches; he also had a longer-term impact on organized itinerant evangelism in Wales, New England, and Nova Scotia. Similarly, Jonathan Edwards (1703-1758) is connected with the English Prayer Call movement and other renewal forces among the Congregationalist and Presbyterian churches in the colonies.[9] Both Whitefield and Edwards emphasized an individual's need to be converted and to be discipled. The unleashed spiritual energy led naturally to tangible forms of Christian service, typically in the form of new voluntary associations.[10]

In the case of the Wesleyan movement, even more specific dependance can be identified. John Wesley, who actually pioneered for modern Anglo-Saxon Christians the notion of outdoor preaching and itinerant evangelism, had a burden for the working classes and underprivileged. A good many people came to hear the gospel from the strategies of the Methodist preachers, and this led Methodism to create numerous avenues of Christian service for its adherents. Even more significant, however, was Wesley's conscious dependance upon the Anglican renewal societies and his own experience as a missionary in the Colony of Georgia with the Society for the Propagation of the Gospel. Shortly after his "Aldersgate Experience" in 1738, Wesley visited the Moravian community at Herrnhut in Saxony and explored their missionary strategies. This led to a Pietistic organizational style in his own fledgling Methodist societies.[11]

---

9. Ernest A. Payne, *The Prayer Call of 1784* (London: Baptist Layman's Missionary Movement, 1941), 1-12.

10. Edwin S. Gaustad, *The Great Awakening in New England* (Chicago: Quadrangle Books, 1968), 25-42, 102ff.; Robert T. Handy, *A History of the Churches in the United States and Canada* (New York: Oxford University Press, 1976), 76-115.

11. See, for instance, J. S. Simon, *John Wesley and the Methodist Societies*

For large numbers of English-speaking Christians, then, there were by the 1780s the necessary yearnings for spiritual renewal, expressed personal needs, and excitement, plus experimenting opportunities for religious voluntarism. The basic voluntary paradigms were in place. Only a catalyst was needed to ignite the general cultural outbreak of voluntarism that some have dubbed an "Age of Associations."

That catalyst was William Carey (1761-1834), who is a watershed for many historians of missions because he pioneered so many ideas and strategies that others used in the nineteenth century. Carey was a devoted student of missionary efforts, particularly those of the Church of England, the Moravians, and the Danish. An egalitarian by nature and social class, Carey devised a plan whereby large numbers of people with modest resources could be involved in the work of missions (for Carey's theological contributions, see Chapter Two). His early success, which occurred concurrent with the beginnings of the Evangelical Revival, demonstrated to others the power and possibilities in mass voluntarism. The Bible society movement, other denominations, and later humanitarian associations learned an important lesson from William Carey's experiment.

"The Missionary Society, Commonly Called the London Missionary Society" (L.M.S.), followed closely on the heels of Carey and the Baptist experience. In September 1795, correspondence from Baptist missionaries led to a general evangelical interest in supporting overseas missions. The London Society became a vehicle for interdenominational involvement as a participatory voluntary association. While the original hope was that Methodists, Congregationalists, Presbyterians, the evangelical wing of the Church of England, and other Independents would join their forces, it was the Congregationalists who predominated and who came to lead the Society. In view of the establishment of general voluntary bodies for missionary

(London: Epworth Press, 1923); D. Pike, "The Religious Societies in the Church of England and Their Influence upon John Wesley" (unpublished M.A. thesis, University of Leeds, 1960); and Henry D. Rack, "Religious Societies and the Origins of Methodism," *Journal of Ecclesiastical History* 38 (1987): 582-95.

endeavour in Glasgow and Edinburgh in 1796, the Society became known as the "London" Society, later fully integrated with the Congregationalist Union. With the establishment of the L.M.S., the overseas voluntary effort among British Christians was well established and defined.

Overseas missions were not the only voluntary result of the resurgence in Christian endeavour amongst British Christians. The growth of itinerant and domestic missions was a powerful force in Wales and the north of England. Although never as attractive a venture as overseas mission to the "heathen," domestic missions, evangelism, and itinerancy were a vital part of the growth of dissent in England at the turn of the nineteenth century. The most obvious results of this effort were the formation of societies and the extension of education. Not only were scores of local and regional voluntary support societies founded, but related projects such as tract distribution caught the attention of promoters as well. By 1830, many more congregations existed than before the effort was undertaken, and the formation of societies had proven its worth as the evangelical organizational technique. Significantly, as recent historians have shown, domestic missions drew rural Christians into the mainstream of national religious concerns.[12]

As the eighteenth century closed, a virtual revolution in Christian action had occurred within British Christianity. Nineteenth-century Christian leaders would reap the benefit of that revolution.[13]

III. The Evangelical Century

As several historians have previously pointed out, the hundred years before the first World War are rightly called the "Evangelical Centu-

---

12. Deryck W. Lovegrove, *Established Church, Sectarian People: Itinerancy and the Transformation of English Dissent, 1780-1830* (Cambridge: Cambridge University Press, 1988), 162-65.

13. For a listing of many of these specific associations, consult William H. Brackney, *Christian Voluntarism in Britain and North America: A Bibliography and Critical Assessment* (Westport, Conn.: Greenwood Press, 1995), 244-57.

ry."[14] Evangelicals, "whose righteousness filled the land," placed their energies in every conceivable area of Christian concern. The voluntary association was a primary vehicle for the Evangelicals, who lacked any other coherent organizational structure and whose sense of Christian endeavour was task oriented. Moreover, voluntarism fit quite nicely with the individualism of the Evangelical conversion experience. It was, in many ways, the combination of a midcentury revival and the growth of an anti-Catholic wing of the Church of England that produced the voluntarist proliferation in Britain in the nineteenth century.[15] Again, it must be emphasized that Evangelicals drew heavily upon the experience and organizational history of earlier churchly voluntarism.

Four emphases of voluntarism were marked among Evangelicals in the latter half of the nineteenth century: the holiness movement, the conservative/liberal debate, evangelistic missions in the Empire, and humanitarian concerns. Each contributed to the plethora of Evangelical associations in Britain.

Perfectionist theology in the United States, as taught by Charles G. Finney (1792-1875) at Oberlin College and practised by evangelist Phoebe Palmer (1817-1874) among the Methodists, was a direct influence upon the holiness tradition in Britain. The movement of individuals and churches that emerged about the 1860s found institutional expression in several kinds of voluntary associations. Premier among them was the Keswick Convention, begun in the English Lake District in 1875; one historian has thought of it as a grand voluntary association of the upper middle class.[16] Others of a regional kind were formed at Cliff College (1884), Star Hall (1889), and the Pentecostal League of 1891. Scores of Christians from the

14. See, for instance, Kathleen Heasman, *Evangelicals in Action: An Appraisal of Their Social Work in the Victorian Era* (London: Geoffrey Bles, 1962), 285-88; Ford K. Brown, *Fathers of the Victorians: The Age of Wilberforce* (Cambridge: Cambridge University Press, 1961), 317.

15. So argued James A. Beckford, "Great Britain: Voluntarism and Sectional Interests," in Robert Wuthnow, ed., *Between States and Markets: The Voluntary Sector in Comparative Perspective* (Princeton, N.J.: Princeton University Press, 1991), 57.

16. David W. Bebbington, *Evangelicalism in Modern Britain: A History from the 1730s to the 1980s* (London: Unwin Hyman, 1989), 177.

Methodist, Brethren, Baptist, Anglican, and Salvation Army traditions (to mention the obvious) participated in the voluntarism of holiness.

A second area that exhibited a pronounced voluntarist tendency well into the early twentieth century was the realignment of theology along the lines of "liberals" and "conservatives." Spurred on by university scholarship and prestigious urban preachers, the issue of biblical authority was a primary theological determinant, and various voluntary associations grew up in response to the issue.[17] Progressive to liberal theologians like F. D. Maurice (1805-1872), Charles Kingsley (1819-1875), and John Clifford (1836-1923) expounded new and critical views that intellectually supported interdenominational cooperation and associations like the Ethical Society (1876), the Christian Education Union (1880), and the Christian Union for Social Service (1876). Among the various approaches of Evangelicals, university scholars like P. T. Forsyth (1848-1921) and the Cambridge Trio of F. J. A. Hort (1828-1892), B. F. Westcott (1825-1901), and J. B. Lightfoot (1828-1889), plus the pulpit ministry of Charles Haddon Spurgeon (1834-1892) and F. B. Meyer (1847-1929) among the Baptists and J. C. Ryle (1816-1900), Anglican Bishop of Liverpool, provided encouragement for a wide variety of voluntary associations, from Spurgeon's local church organizations to Keswick and the Protestant Truth Society. Also in the universities and among the churches, missionary and study societies, such as the Intercollegiate Christian Union (1877) and the Bible League (1892), grew up in support of the new evangelical concerns.

The British Empire provided a ready field of interest for Victorian Evangelicals. In India, a dozen associations were formed between 1848 and 1876, the more memorable being the North India Book and Tract Society (1848) and the Bengal Evangelistic Mission (1874). Likewise China was a favoured recipient, with at least ten associations formed in the nineteenth century; noteworthy were the Society for the Diffusion of Useful Knowledge in China (1830) and the Education Association of China (1890). Of special interest to Victorians were the Jews, both in Britain and in Palestine. Missions to the Jews included publication of tracts, direct evangelistic appeals,

17. A good survey of the intellectual ferment is found in Bebbington, 105-51.

and support of converted Jews who laboured in various trades and professions. Associations particularly dedicated to Jewish work included the Prayer Union for Israel (1880), the Palestine and Lebanon Nurses Association (1887), and the Hebrew Christian Testimony to Israel (1894).

Humanitarian efforts spanned a wide variety among Evangelicals. Societies were formed to assist the reformation of ladies of the night, to retrain chimney sweeps, to provide care for incurables, to encourage abstinence and temperance with respect to alcoholic consumption, to encourage good reading habits, and to look after chaperons for courting females. Among the prominent organizations were the British and Foreign Temperance Society (1831), the Charitable and Provident Society for Granting Pensions to the Aged and Infirmed Deaf and Dumb (1836), the Workhouse Visiting Society (1858), and the Homes for the Aged Poor (1869).

Perhaps the grandest achievements of the Evangelical leaders were the Evangelical Alliance and the Exeter Hall Meetings. Formed in 1846, the Alliance was a voluntary union of individual Christians of different churches. The Alliance fostered religious liberty, cooperation among the churches, and a renewed sense of the value of missions.[18] Exeter Hall became in 1833 the marketplace of Evangelical associations to hold their annual meetings and display their literature and programmes, as well as a forum for great preachers like Charles Haddon Spurgeon. The Hall event lasted into the late 1890s.[19]

Evangelicals per se, however, were not the sole exponents of voluntarism in Victorian Britain. Churchly bodies also emerged in significant numbers. Anglicans formed over thirty-five voluntary associations in areas as diverse as seaman's missions, children's work, and religious women. The Society of Friends formed societies to work among prisoners and medical missions. Unitarians began in 1874 a social Purity Alliance, and Presbyterians, Meth-

18. The Alliance is more fully discussed in Chapter Five.

19. There is no contemporary study of this grand event. See Frederick M. Holmes, *Exeter Hall and Its Associations* (London: Hodder and Stoughton, 1881), for a survey of the early years.

odists, and Congregationalists commenced various sorts of urban and overseas mission associations. Church-related voluntarism constituted a significant bloc of the voluntary associations formed by British Christians.

In the twentieth century, Christian voluntarism in Britain radiated from three foci. First was the coalition of ecumenical missionary interests, exemplified in the International Missionary Council in 1905. Scores of sending, support, and consultative associations include the Action Partners — Christians Reaching Around the World (1904), Evangelical Missionary Alliance (1958), and the Council for World Mission (1977). Next were those midcentury organizations devoted to humanitarian needs: Christian Action (1943), Christian Aid (1945), and the distantly religious Oxford Famine Relief Committee (1942), and more recently, Feed the Minds (1963) and Christian Outreach (1967). Christian Action, a pioneer, originally focussed on the relief of Germany after World War II, but later shifted its concern to political issues like opposing apartheid in South Africa. A third focus has been interest/affinity groups related to Christianity in its broadest aspects. Those associations, now over one hundred in number, include a wide variety: Optical Christian Fellowship (1960), Ecclesiastical History Society (1961), a scholarly professional association, Caravanners and Campers Christian Fellowship (1969), Fellowship of Christian Motorcyclists (1976), Christians in Sport (1976), the Lesbian and Gay Christian Movement (1976), Clergy Against Nuclear Arms (1982), and the Christian Dance Fellowship (1990).

The great flurry of voluntary organizations that occurred in Britain during the "Evangelical Century" was to be a high-water mark of voluntary endeavour. The growth of government responsibility for social concerns, the numerical demise of the churches, and the surviving success and institutionalization of many British voluntary associations all contributed to a slowing of voluntary organization in the twentieth century. However, in the last two decades, partly in response to North American organizational outreach, hundreds of new voluntary Christian associations have sprung up, filling a nine hundred–page directory. Several British associations such as Spring Harvest, a charismatic renewal fellowship that started in 1979 at

Prestatyn, Wales, attract thousands of adherents and raise millions of pounds annually.[20]

Summary

British churchly Christians pioneered the patterns, proliferated the associations, and watched as denominational voluntarism was transformed into other forms of Christian endeavour. Voluntarism was peculiar to Christianity in Great Britain because of a very old Nonconformist tendency. When the opportunity arrived in the seventeenth century to create new organizational patterns under Toleration, churchmen and Nonconformists alike rose to the challenge. Patterns were borrowed unashamedly from commerce and the guilds, and virtually every segment of society had a role to play. From Henry Ashurst and John Locke to William Carey and Thomas Chalmers, a long and distinguished list of apologists for voluntarism rationalized theologically and practically the need and benefits of Christian voluntarism. Finally, what began in the Church to expand and critique Christian action moved beyond the Church to a wide variety of humanitarian causes and later parachurch organizations across British culture. This was the ultimate impact of a movement that began as the religious outgrowth of a commercial venture in 1649.

20. Various organizations have produced the annual *U.K. Christian Handbook*, ed. Peter Brierley and Heather Wraight (London: Christian Research, 1996), an invaluable tool for economic and demographic data.

CHAPTER FOUR

North American Developments

I. The Earliest Efforts

Religious voluntarism came to the Americas via European Christianity. As mission efforts in the Old World sought converts in the New beginning in the late seventeenth century, in the British colonial tradition it was primarily via the voluntary association, both churchly and independent. In what became the United States, the "voluntary way" was the principal expression of Christian growth and religious organizational expansion. Both churchly and nonaligned Christianity used voluntary strategies, as did extraordinary movements considered out of the mainstream. Voluntarism was, as Robert Baird (1798-1863), an early American church historian, described it, the result of American energy and self-reliance, a privilege of self-help in a country that enjoyed great blessings and opportunities.[1]

North American voluntarism began, as in Britain, within the circles of the churches. Following a pattern set by English (particularly Anglican) associations, the oldest religious voluntary associations in British North America were missionary and focussed upon the evangelization of the Indians and the planting of congregations.[2]

---

1. Robert Baird, *Religion in America, or An Account of the Origin, Relation to the State, and Recent Condition of the Evangelical Churches in the United States, with Notices of Unevangelical Denominations* (New York: Harper Brothers, 1856), 365-67.
2. For a summary of the earliest missionary efforts, see Charles L. Chaney, *The Birth of Missions in America* (Pasadena, Calif.: William Carey Library, 1976),

The New York Missionary Society, founded in 1796, is a paradigm of many.[3] Presbyterians, the Reformed Church, Baptists, and others joined in this effort to assist missions to the Six Nations of the Niagara frontier. The strategy for a cooperative effort arose out of the normal patterns of Christian ministry in the New York urban context and for about a decade (1796-1806) worked quite well. The interest in missions among the Six Nations stemmed from earlier New England efforts among the Indians and from western New York homesteaders' need to have a settled frontier. The ideal of an ecumenical missionary society lasted until 1807, when an appointed Baptist missionary of the society, Elkanah Holmes (1744-1832), decided he should advocate a strictly confessional position on the matter of believer's baptism. At that point, in support of Holmes, a new voluntary association of solely Baptists was born.

In New York, Boston, and Philadelphia, then, with numerous examples and modest support from the ecclesiastical structures of Britain, American colonial Christians took the direction of the culture and created structures that fitted the need. Such associations were simple in structure, with the few necessary officers. They possessed highly focussed objectives, almost always singular in number. Meetings were at least annual and democratic decision making prevailed.

The full blossoming of America's voluntary tradition was concurrent with the rise of evangelicalism at the turn of the nineteenth century. The great revivalists — notably those in New England and on the frontier — stressed the need for conversion and capability. The average person came to see that he/she had gifts fit for God's work and an inherent obligation to use them. Spurred on by the British Baptists' and Congregationalists' interest in overseas missions, Americans came to own the conversion of the world as their ideal. It became fashionable for "every man" to engage in mission, and the

---

101-36. Chaney assumes a "Puritan ribwork" as the foundation for the missionary impulse in the colonial United States.

3. Among the earlier associations were Society of the United Brethren for Propagating the Gospel Among the Heathen (1745); Society for the Propagation of Christianity and Useful Knowledge Among the Germans in America (1773); American Society for Propagating the Gospel Among the Indians and Others in North America (1787).

entire life of the churches was transformed. Baptists had long utilized their associational principle, largely imitating the work of the Congregationalists. What was truly startling was the engagement of the voluntary principle among Episcopalians and Lutherans.

One of the profound results of early North American Christian experience was the legitimation of "denominational Christianity." In both the United States and Canada, fostered by the vast frontier, where countless varieties of religious associations flourished, from mission congregations of mainstream Protestantism and Roman Catholicism to communes like the Amana Society or the Rappites, denominational understanding led to a toleration of each other's right to maintain one's religious position. This was undergirded in the United States Constitution by the First Amendment, "Congress shall make no laws concerning an establishment of religion."[4] Even the Old World faiths came to coexist with each other and understand that the Kingdom of God was broad and inclusive indeed. By the first decades of the nineteenth century, the denominations themselves were behaving in a voluntarist fashion, erupting organizationally, responding to rapid change, and promoting highly individualistic forms of Christian experience.[5]

Perhaps the greatest examples of the voluntarist behaviour of denominations were the "come-outer" groups (sometimes referred to as the "smaller sects"[6]) like the Freewill Baptists, the Cumberland Presbyterians, and the Churches of Christ. The Freewill Baptists sprang up in New England between 1780 and 1825 as a reaction to the theological determinism and social elitism of the Congregationalists and Calvinistic Regular Baptists. They emphasized "free grace, free will, and free communion." The Cumberland Presbyteri-

---

4. *The Declaration of Independence and the Constitution of the United States* (New York: Book of the Month Club, 1976), 16.

5. As Bryan Wilson has shown, one of the principal features of a denomination is that it is formally a voluntary association. See his *Patterns of Sectarianism: Organisation and Ideology in Social and Religious Movements* (London: Heinemann, 1967), 25.

6. Wilson, at 23ff., uses a modified typology to argue that a primary characteristic of the sect is that it is a voluntary association where, among other attributes, "there is opportunity for the member spontaneously to express his commitment."

ans arose in the Appalachian Mountains of Kentucky and Tennessee at the turn of the nineteenth century as the institutionalization of the Great Revivals that began at Cane Ridge in 1800. In a period of discord in the Christian Church (Disciples of Christ) involving issues of instrumental music in worship, church societies, and the ordinances, several hundred congregations left the mainstream Campbell-Stone movement and formed a loose confederation called the "Churches of Christ." Denominationalism in America became an opportunity to increase the variety of Christians just by starting a new category and legitimating the position by building a following and creating a viable association.

Part of the dynamic of this denominational voluntarism was "sacred competition." The "come-outers" found their greatest success among those left behind by the Old World religions: the Lutherans, Anglicans, Reformed churches, and the Roman Catholics. The "come-outer" grassroots organization was typically voluntary to the core and revivalistic in nature. This proved highly effective on the frontier, in the urban immigrant communities, and among the African-American population. "Winning people to Christ" became the watchword in western regions that were described as "godless communities of infidelism and debauchery," in the cities where "popery raised its foreign head," and, in the case of the slave population, among a race of "unevangelized, benighted people." From about 1820 through the 1880s, the targets of the evangelical denominations, and the "come-outers" in particular, were Oregon and California, the east coast and Ohio Valley cities, and the southern black communities, first slave, then free.[7] Concern over the growth of these sects among these populations led Episcopalians and Lutherans in particular to adopt their own strategies. They too realized the fervor of the evangelical crusade and its overall results in the life of the denominations. Thus

7. Edwin S. Gaustad, ed., *A Documentary History of Religion in America,* vol. I (Grand Rapids, Mich.: Eerdmans, 1982), 382-97; Sydney E. Ahlstrom, *A Religious History of the American People* (New Haven: Yale University Press, 1972), 472-91. Robert T. Handy, *A History of the Churches in the United States and Canada* (New York: Oxford University Press, 1976), 208-10, comments upon the impact of Protestantism in the black community.

the Domestic and Foreign Missionary Society of the Protestant Episcopal Church was created in 1820, followed by a Central Lutheran Missionary Society in 1835. By 1845, the Baptist denomination in America (in some ways the voluntary principle par excellence) was an interlocking network of over sixty-five voluntary associations.[8]

Some American Christians resisted the temptation to create voluntary associations as long as they could. Alexander Campbell (1788-1866) and Barton W. Stone (1772-1844) had been abused by associations of both Baptists and Presbyterians in their early careers, and they held tenaciously to the independence of local churches and only biblically sanctioned extra-parish bodies in their ecclesiology.[9] By the 1840s, however, even Campbell had come to realize the trend of denominational growth in the United States: "We can do little in the great missionary field of the world either at home or abroad without cooperation . . . we can have no thorough cooperation without a more ample, extensive, and thorough church organization."[10] Distrust of the voluntary organizing principle beyond the local congregation had been turned into affirmation.

The earliest form of religious voluntarism in the United States was thus denominational, and this was followed by cooperation among the denominations. A point that has not been sufficiently emphasized in the historiography either of American religion or of separate denominations is the high degree of cooperation in denominational voluntary associations beginning in the 1820s. The first form of cooperation was among regional bodies within a confessional tradition: Baptist associations united to form conventions; Congregationalists worked together through associations and in the Board

---

8. William H. Brackney, *Christian Voluntarism in Britain and North America: A Bibliography and Critical Assessment* (Westport, Conn.: Greenwood Press, 1995), 266-68.

9. For a sociological analysis of the organizational evolution of the Disciples of Christ, see Oliver R. Whitley, "The Sect to Denomination Process in an American Religious Movement: The Disciples of Christ," *Southwestern Social Science Quarterly* 36 (1955): 275-82.

10. *Millennial Harbinger,* 1842, 523; Lester G. McAllister and William E. Tucker, *Journey in Faith: A History of the Christian Church (Disciples of Christ)* (St. Louis, Mo.: Bethany Press), 170ff.

of Commissioners of Foreign Missions; and Lutherans acted in concert with the Germantown, Pennsylvania, Synod. Two overpowering reasons for intradenominational cooperation were domestic missions (church planting and itinerant ministry) and education.

The Bible society movement was the germ of interdenominational voluntary cooperation. It did not require the permission of denominational organizations to form and operate. Rather, it drew upon the leadership of individuals from many denominations to shape its own agenda around the Scriptures. The first Bible associations were formed between 1800 and 1810 in the northeastern urban areas: Boston, southern Maine, the Connecticut coastal towns, and New York. Based on the success of the British and Foreign Bible Society, several local organizations joined efforts in 1816 to cooperate nationally. The Bible society movement taught American Protestants what they had in common.

American Congregationalists were the first to experiment with interdenominational voluntarism for missionary purposes. In Boston and New York, the urban environment had brought forth local missionary societies, and in the establishment of the Plan of Union in 1801, the Congregationalists showed they were prepared to cooperate with Presbyterians.[11] This undoubtedly laid a foundation for Philadelphia Presbyterians and New England Congregationalists and others in the Reformed theological tradition to create the American Board of Commissioners for Foreign Missions in 1813. This board became the parent of all the cooperative voluntary mission associations at the national level. Soon thereafter came the American Education Society (1815), the American Colonization Society and the American Sunday School Union (1817), the American Seaman's Friend Society (1820), the American Tract Society (1825), and the American Home Missionary Society (1826), just to mention the principal national cooperative associations.[12] In these ventures, the primary denominational participants were Congregationalists, Presbyterians, branches of the Reformed Churches, and sometimes Bap-

---

11. The Plan is printed in Williston Walker, *The Creeds and Platforms of Congregationalism* (Boston: Pilgrim Press, 1960), 530-31.

12. A comprehensive listing is found in Brackney, 259ff.

tists and Lutherans. To protect the necessary denominational interests, board members and officers of the great national bodies were carefully chosen to reflect denominational diversity, as in the American Tract Society.[13] Leaders like Lyman Beecher, Albert Barnes, Adoniram Judson, and Samuel Schmucker all heralded from differing confessions a new era of cooperation in which "great fundamentals of holy religion are held in common by all."[14]

Following on the success of the mainstream denominations and the great national societies were the independent voluntary religious associations in the United States. Then came the independent forms, chiefly associated with various forms of evangelical expression. One root of the independents was the immigrant church, like the German Methodists, German Baptists, and various bodies of Lutherans. These subcategories of the mainstream Protestant consensus created both domestic and foreign missionary societies, as well as using the voluntary principle to start colleges and seminaries. Another root was the holiness tradition, an outgrowth of the Second Great Awakening and the revivals of the 1850s, particularly evident among Methodists. Holiness associations and camp meeting associations cropped up across the United States following the Civil War.[15]

In the seventh and eighth decades of the nineteenth century, a number of cooperative, independent voluntary associations for missionary purposes were started. Urban missions in Washington, New York, and Chicago drew large numbers of Christian supporters from several churches, but were not affiliated with any ecclesiastical body. Overseas missionary societies, like China Inland Mission (1865), the Christian and Missionary Alliance (1887), Central American Mission

13. Winthrop S. Hudson, *Religion in America: An Historical Account of the Development of American Religious Life* (New York: Scribner's, 1973), 153.

14. Quoted in Sidney E. Mead, "The Rise of the Evangelical Conception of Ministry in America: 1607-1850," in H. R. Niebuhr and Daniel D. Williams, eds., *The Ministry in Historical Perspective* (New York: Harper and Row, 1981), 223-26.

15. For the organizational background of the holiness tradition, see Timothy L. Smith, *Revivalism and Social Reform in Mid-Nineteenth Century America* (New York: Abingdon Press, 1957); on the camp meeting movement, consult Melvin E. Dieter, *The Holiness Revival of the Nineteenth Century* (Metuchen, N.J.: Scarecrow Press, 1980).

(1890), the Pocket Testament League (1893), and the Venezuela Mission (1895) illustrated the evangelical tradition. Others in a more liberal theological stance included the Christian labour movement (1870s), the Institutional Church League, and the New York Federation of Churches and Christian Workers (1895). Student missions were also prominent in the independent category, reflecting both the evangelical ethos (Young People's Society of Christian Endeavor, 1881) and the theologically evolving Student Volunteer Movement for Foreign Missions (1888). Although frequently beyond the constituencies of mainstream Protestants, and unaffiliated with any ecclesiastical body, these independent voluntary mission associations followed scrupulously the models of denominational voluntarism achieved earlier in the century.

II. Voluntarist Humanitarianism

As several historians have shown, the experience among the churches with voluntary associations quickly lent itself to other forms of Christian endeavour. A humanitarian impulse among Baptists in the North led to the establishment of antislavery societies, first among the Freewill Baptists (1842), the next year among Regular Baptists. The American Baptist Free Mission Society, Congregationalists, Presbyterians, and Unitarians pioneered in the formation of the American Antislavery Society in 1832; and Christians with experience in tract distribution, Sunday Schools, evangelism, and Bible publication went beyond the blessing of their denominations and formed non-aligned associations, often in competition with the denominationally sanctioned associations. Two examples of this "voluntary spinoff" were the American Missionary Association (1841), an antislavery group interested in missions with southern slaves, and the American Bible Union (1850), a collection of biblical purists.

An interesting feature of mid-nineteenth-century voluntarism was the association of a negative or socially restrictive kind. An early form of this behaviour was the antimasonic movement that erupted in New York State in a crusade to outlaw and abolish Freemasonry from the United States. Clubs, church associations, and religiopolitical coalitions joined in this effort from 1828 to the 1870s.[16] Later, another manifestation of negative voluntarism was seen among various Protestant groups that attempted to restrict Roman Catholics from political office and to ostracize them from neighbourhood developments. Chief among these were the Orange Lodge Movement (1824) and the American Protestant Union formed in 1842, the latter to a certain extent resuscitated in 1887 with the American Protective Association.[17] On a racial/ethnic basis was the Ku Klux Klan, formed in 1865 among socially radical groups in the American South and Midwest, with definite religious bases to their programme of white supremacy and reduction of black social mobility and privileges.

During and after the American Civil War, Christian voluntarism was especially concerned with the American South. At first, new associations like the United States Sanitary Commission (1861) and the United States Christian Commission (1861) were started to assist in meeting the spiritual and physical needs of those in the military situation. Later, Protestant groups formed associations like the American Christian Association (1868) to build institutions for the freed slave population. Certain of the denominations encouraged the growth of voluntary associations among blacks. The Baptists were a good example of this in fostering education societies, missionary bodies, and literacy bands to enhance the religious communities of the black population. Congregationalists and others joined older societies like the American Missionary Association (1841) with a renewed purpose, to launch many educational and self-help projects.

American cities provided a fruitful arena for voluntary endeavour of varying sorts. Issues in the urban environment included housing shortages, poor sanitation, inadequate schools, assimilation of new immigrants, crime, and employment regulation. Church-related and independent voluntary organizations together and in competition arose to meet the needs. Among the churches, the

---

16. Alice Felt Tyler, *Freedom's Ferment: Phases of American Social History from the Colonial Period to the Outbreak of the Civil War* (New York: Harper and Row, 1962), 351-95.

17. Ray Allen Billington, *The Protestant Crusade 1800-1860: A Study of the Origins of American Nativism* (Chicago: Quadrangle Books, 1962), 166-93.

Methodists established church extension societies and city missions, and Baptists created "fresh air societies" in the 1870s and 1880s; the Episcopalians started a Christian Social Union in 1891; and the Roman Catholics worked through various ethnic associations and the St. Vincent de Paul Society. Even more impressive as voluntary associations were the independent and/or Evangelical city missions (the first of which seems to have been in Boston in 1867), and national organizations like the Young Men's Christian Association (1850) and its female counterpart (1858), and later the Christian Industrial League (1893) and the Institutional Church League (1894). Many church coalitions like the Christian Industrial Alliance (1890) and the Oberlin Institute of Christian Sociology (1894) joined forces with governments and higher education to formulate social science strategies for urban improvement.

No other area of voluntary expansion better illustrates the pulse beat of American religious life in the late nineteenth century than women's work. Largely an outgrowth of local women's missionary support societies from earlier in the century, in the 1870s and 1880s over two dozen associations of women for mission were formed inside and outside the traditional denominational structures. Initially, these organizations were formed to send women in their own right to mission work at home and abroad; later many of these denominational bodies sought cooperation with each other and a new kind of ecumenical voluntarism emerged. Baptist women organized from 1871 to 1888, Methodists from 1869 to 1894, Episcopalians and Presbyterians from 1871 to 1882, and Lutherans in 1884. Roman Catholics organized their first ladies' aid society in 1887, and the Catholic-affiliated Hibernian Society created a women's auxiliary in the following year. The ecumenical-style voluntary association was first seen in seaman's friend societies in the 1850s and Indian work in the 1880s. Major ecumenical advances were made with the Women's Union Missionary Society of America (1860), the first to appoint single women missionaries overseas, and the Women's Christian Temperance Union (1874), the most extensive network of ecumenical women's organizations.[18]

18. For a listing of the specific associations founded in the United States and Canada before 1900, consult Brackney, 260-77.

III. New Directions for a New Century

The new century witnessed ecumenical voluntarism, particularly in the area of student missions. In 1886, the Student Volunteer Movement for Foreign Missions was formed at Mt. Hermon, California, and spread quickly to Britain and Europe. In a similar vein, the British-born Student Christian Movement reached the United States in the 1890s, and a strong network was achieved among American universities. Theological differences within British S.C.M. circles led to the ultimate establishment of InterVarsity in the United States in 1941, which has flourished among evangelical students throughout the century. Similar to InterVarsity U.S. are the Navigators, formed in 1933 by Dawson Trotman (1906-1956) to work among servicemen and on campuses and in high schools, Percy Crawford's (1902-1960) Youth for Christ (1930), Pioneer Clubs (1939), Young Life (1941), and Campus Crusade for Christ, founded in 1951 by evangelist Bill Bright (1921-).

It is difficult to classify many of the churchly manifestations of the ecumenical movement in the United States as purely voluntary, primarily because many are supported and administered by ecclesiastical processes. However, several regional organizations and some national ecumenical movements display voluntary tendencies. Urban councils of churches and their regional counterparts, which may focus upon celebrations of unity (a community Thanksgiving service) and humanitarian projects (a food cupboard), fit the voluntary tradition. Also, the Lord's Day Alliance (1888), the World Day of Prayer (probably first celebrated in 1890), and the partly voluntary Religion in American Life (1949) illustrate the voluntary attraction of Christian unity as an impetus to ecumenical behaviour. Several denominational relief organizations, like the Mennonite Voluntary Service, enjoy ecumenical voluntary support. An example of a highly focussed ecumenical voluntary association is the Hymn Society of the United States and Canada (1922), which publishes music and provides support for church musicians and authors.

The irenic spirit of American evangelical Christians is likewise demonstrated in the establishment of the American Council of Christian Churches (a 1941 fundamentalist reaction to the Federal Council of Churches) and the National Association of Evangelicals (1942), a milder form of conservative theological activism. Since the Second World War, a wide variety of theologically conservative (mostly Protestant) voluntary associations have emerged, including the Christian Doctors Sodality (1924), a medical practitioner's referral service and fellowship; the American Scientific Affiliation (1941), which provides a forum for various scientists to publish their faith-related concerns; the Evangelical Theological Society (1949), a professional scholars' coalition; the Fellowship of Christian Athletes (1954), which organizes committed athletes and sports chaplains; and Cowboys for Christ (1971), which focuses upon a Christian witness in the livestock industry.

In the later decades of the twentieth century new forms of religious voluntarism have arisen in the United States. One type is related to political activism: the Americans United for Separation of Church and State (P.O.A.U.), the National Association of Religious Broadcasters, and the Moral Majority, Inc., which translate religious perspective into political activism. Another form is the organizational network manifested around mass evangelism. First on the radio were Charles Fuller (1887-1968) with the "Old Time Revival Hour," M. R. De Haan (1891-1965) with the "Radio Bible Class," and Billy Graham (1918-) with the "Hour of Decision." Later with the advent of television, Oral Roberts (1918-), Rex Humbard (1919-), Robert Schuller (1926-), Jerry Falwell (1933-), and countless others have all established "prayer partners" of voluntary supporters who contribute to a ministry, receive its literature, follow its agenda, and identify as its association.[19]

American Evangelicals are by no means the only theologically distinct Christians to have noticed the value of voluntary association. Social activist groups within the churches as well as freestanding associations of concern have long populated the lists of American religious voluntary associations. For instance, beginning in the 1960s within the mainline Protestant denominations, caucuses grew up in

19. On the radio and televangelists in general, see Quentin J. Schultze, ed., *American Evangelicals and the Mass Media* (Grand Rapids, Mich.: Zondervan Publishing Co., 1990).

support of gay/lesbian identity. Dignity/U.S.A. (1968), a Roman Catholic association; American Baptists Concerned (1972); Interweave (1971), related to the Unitarian Universalist Churches; United Church Coalition for Lesbian/Gay Concerns (1973); and Affirmation/Gay Lesbian Mormons (1977), to mention a few, have constituted themselves as formal, permanent voluntary associations largely to educate their churches to homosexual issues and to provide various forums for fellowship. By 1995, over twenty-six Christian associations had registered in support of gay/lesbian issues. Other socially activist voluntary associations include the National Conference of Christians and Jews (1928), which builds better human relations among its constituents, and the Christian Chaplain Service (1926), which provides volunteers to prison inmates.

Because of a long-standing voluntary tradition, Americans have an inherent tendency to use the voluntary principle in its broadest religious applications.

IV. The Voluntary Experience in Canada

Canadian Christian voluntarism was substantially different from the American experience and warrants separate discussion. What differentiates Canadian voluntarism from that in the United States is the peculiar heritage of the leading Protestant denominations of the nineteenth century. A quasi-establishment situation bred a reaction from those considered revivalistic in the American sense and those considered dissenting in the British sense. As one writer has observed, "Canadian voluntarists seem to have been directly motivated by resentment against preferential treatment for denominations that failed to earn it by their missionary zeal."[20]

The leading Protestant churches entering the British North American provinces in the early nineteenth century were the Church of England, the Church of Scotland, the Free Church, the Presbyterian Church in Canada, and several branches of Method-

---

20. John Webster Grant, *The Church in the Canadian Era* (Toronto: McGraw Hill Ryerson, 1972), 14.

ism: British Wesleyan Methodists, American Episcopal Methodists, and Bible Christians. Baptists joined the mix in at least four manifestations: Regular Calvinistic Baptists from the United States, British Union Baptists, Scotch Baptists or Haldanites, and the Freewill Baptists from New England. "Territoriality" was a strong influence among the older European bodies, and this led to a tradition of deep confessional loyalties.

The Anglican Church and, to a lesser extent, certain Presbyterian groups attempted to establish themselves as the official status churches in various regions. Roman Catholic interests, loyal to the British Crown, also reminded the government of their position. The more "evangelical" groups, particularly the Regular Baptists and several branches of Methodists, fought for recognition of status for clergy and property against what came to be called the "family compact," an Anglican elite that controlled religious policy in the colony. In the late 1830s this struggle led to a major political confrontation over the sale of clergy lands and the establishment of higher education in the province of Upper Canada.[21]

Baptists like Robert A. Fyfe (1816-1878) and Methodists like A. Egerton Ryerson (1803-1882) advocated what came to be known as the "voluntary system" of support for church institutions. By this was meant that each church tradition was responsible for the funding of its own institutions — this strict voluntary position was the stance of most Baptists, doubtless under the influence of American Baptists.[22] Many Methodists joined the Baptists, while some in the British Wesleyan group accepted grants for missions and were willing to support the interests of the Established Church. In the 1830s, Presbyterians, Roman Catholics, and Methodists argued convincingly for a broader distribution of the land sale proceeds to assist church-related institutions. What resulted was the "semi-voluntary" plan,

21. The best monograph on the topic is Alan Wilson, *The Clergy Reserves in Upper Canada* (Ottawa: Canadian Historical Association, 1969).

22. See above, Chapter Two, 40-41. Fyfe's influence on voluntarist public policy has not been fully appreciated. Fyfe was trained in the United States and travelled extensively there among the Baptist community. See Theo T. Gibson, *Robert Alexander Fyfe: His Contemporaries and His Influence* (Burlington, Ont.: G. R. Welch, 1988), 34-63.

whereby denominations had complete control over their institutions while also receiving support from a benevolent government in proportion to the amount each church raised by its own exertions.[23]

Most of the voluntary associations that emerged in the Canadian nineteenth-century experience were church-related. The largest category of associations was devoted to missions, and many of these were auxiliary for many years to either British or American associations. The Bible society movement in Canada (see Chapter Five) illustrates the dependence of the Canadian organization on the British and Foreign Bible Society until 1905. Some important examples of humanitarian effort and special concerns also developed, notably the Women's Christian Temperance Union (1874) and an Antislavery Society (1851).

The formation of voluntary associations in the Canadian provinces in the late nineteenth century followed predictable patterns of the British and American kinds, though the American models seem to have predominated. British missionary groups formed Canadian auxiliaries, notably the S.P.G. and the S.P.C.K. among the Anglicans, the Wesleyan Methodist Missionary Society among Methodists, and the Glasgow Colonial Society among Presbyterians. More importantly to the course of Canadian voluntarism, evangelical influences helped create voluntary organizations inside the churches — the lay Brotherhood Movement from England — and outside the ecclesiastical accountabilities — the Young People's Society of Christian Endeavor from the United States. Women's organized voluntary mission societies appeared in virtually all of the mainstream Protestant groups in Canada, beginning in the 1870s. American women had a profound influence on Canadian organizations.[24]

Canadian religious voluntarism at the turn of the century also

23. The final plan was inspired by a plan used in New South Wales. See John S. Moir, *The Church in the British Era: From the British Conquest to Confederation* (Toronto: McGraw Hill Ryerson, 1972), 122-25.

24. For an excellent survey of various forms of voluntarism among women, consult Elizabeth G. Muir and Marilyn Fardig Whiteley, eds., *Changing Roles of Women Within the Christian Church in Canada* (Toronto: University of Toronto Press, 1995), and Gloria Neufeld Redekop, *The Work of Their Hands: Mennonite Women's Societies in Canada* (Waterloo, Ont.: Wilfred Laurier Press, 1996).

exhibited reforming and socially strategic tendencies. One of the most popular grassroots voluntary associations was the temperance society. Local and regional organizations produced national bodies in the "reordering process" of the 1880s. The national consciousness of the "His Dominion" movement also provided a vehicle for city missions and national organizations of lay initiative like the Lord's Day Alliance.[25] Important to millions of immigrants were the Roman Catholic fraternal voluntary associations like the Ancient Order of Hibernians (1887) and the Knights of St. John (1892), and the revitalized Orange Lodge movement among certain Protestants.[26] Of social significance, but with a definite religious basis, were the deaconess chapters and sisterhoods of the Anglican and Lutheran churches and eventually, in the new century, the Movement for a Christian Social Order (1931), primarily within the United Church of Canada. Canadians, mostly in the Prairie provinces, exhibited noticeable tendencies toward the Ku Klux Klan, imitating American racial attitudes.

The Prairie provinces in the twentieth century provide a fascinating example of nascent Canadian voluntarism. William Aberhart (1878-1943), a theologically self-educated pastor and Bible expositor in Alberta, recognized the possibilities of expanding his ministry through the use of radio. In 1925 Aberhart began his Radio Sunday School, and he soon claimed hundreds of adherents. Recognizing his need to coalesce his diffuse support, he organized the Westbourne Prophetic Bible Institute Association, out of which grew the first Bible college in the Canadian West. Aberhart's ministry eventually extended to journalism and publication with a political agenda, and it formed a voluntary paradigm for the region.[27]

25. A good discussion of the era is in George A. Rawlyk, ed., *The Canadian Protestant Experience 1760-1990* (Burlington, Ont., 1990), 120ff.

26. On the Catholic associations, see Brian P. Clarke, "Piety, Nationalism, and Fraternity: The Rise of Irish Catholic Voluntary Associations in Toronto, 1850-1895" (unpublished Ph.D. dissertation, University of Chicago, 1986). The Orange Lodge story is told in Hereward Senior, "The Genesis of Canadian Orangeism," *Ontario History* 60 (1968): 13-29.

27. L. P. V. Johnson and Ola J. MacNutt, *Aberhart of Alberta* (Edmonton, Alb.: Institute of Applied Art, 1970), 63-73; David R. Elliott and Iris Miller, *Bible Bill: A Biography of William Aberhart* (Edmonton, Alb.: Reidmore, 1987).

In the later decades of the twentieth century, as church bodies and associations across Canada sought to "Canadianize" themselves, many voluntary associations have strengthened their national identities. Tax laws and charitable donation status in Canada differ from the United States, and this has led to differing understandings of how voluntary associations receive support. In recent years, with satellite communications technology so readily available, the Canadian Christian community has been included in most voluntary appeals of American televangelists and Christian associations. Typically, American-based ministries use a Canadian address and tax identification number.

Moreover, Canadian evangelicals of the later twentieth century have shaped their own voluntary mass ministries. Building on the example of Oswald J. Smith (1889-1986) in Toronto, who created in 1926 the "Back Home Hour" weekly radio broadcasts, are David Mainse's (1936-) "100 Huntley Street" of Burlington, Ontario, telecasts (similar to Pat Robertson's [1930-] "700 Club" and the Christian Broadcasting Network in Virginia Beach, Virginia) and Terry Winter's religious conversation telecasts, which have created a regular list of voluntary "partners," not unlike the Trinity Broadcasting Network in the U.S.

Summary

In general, the voluntary way in church support and the spontaneous voluntary associationalism of every conceivable form of Christianity in the United States and Canada is the dominant motif of North American Christianity. As in the British tradition, voluntary Christianity in North America had its origins within churchly Christianity and later influenced a watershed of other Christian expressions. It is important to underscore the stages through which North American Christian voluntarism developed: (1) a denominational experiment, (2) denominational cooperation, and (3) independent spontaneous Christian endeavour. The vastness of territory, the frontier opportunity, the sense of competition rooted in individualism, and the expectation of the millennium being fulfilled in a New World have all ensured that religious voluntarism among an enlightened people was the preferred vehicle of Christian advance.

CHAPTER FIVE

Internal and External Patterns of Voluntarism

Voluntary associations behave historically like other organizations: they pass through typical life cycles and they regenerate into other forms, influencing yet other voluntary associations. This chapter will examine the life cycle of a typical religious voluntary association and demonstrate the functions of associations in their religious and social contexts.

I. The Life Cycle of an Association

Organizational sociologists have long recognized that organizations move through natural, predictable stages in their development. This particular aspect of organizational sociology was noted in the work of R. C. Angell[1] and more recently in J. O. Hertzler. Hertzler in particular asserted that institutions do not evolve in a regular and sequential process. Instead, their development is tangled and often exhibits time gaps between stages of development.[2] While organizational development is irregular, it is possible to draw generalizations

---

1. C. H. Cooley, R. C. Angell, and L. J. Carr, *Introductory Sociology* (New York: Scribner's, 1933), 406-13.
2. J. O. Hertzler, *Social Institutions* (Lincoln, Neb.: University of Nebraska Press, 1946), 82.

and apply the hypotheses to voluntary associations. Records do exist in abundance for countless organizations of the past, and many contemporary groups are also worthy of careful observation. Curiously, not much serious sociological analysis has taken place in the area of voluntary associations.

Social scientists have observed, therefore, that associations pass through four predictable stages: incipient, efficient, formal, and disorganization.[3] During the incipient phase, the association is formed by a close circle of people around either an urgent objective or a charismatic leader. Identifying the membership, sharpening a definition of the purpose of the association, and sustaining interest are the main energies of the leaders. Voluntary activity is high and is expressed as participation in the decision-making processes of the association. As Hertzler suggested, the origin of an association may be either spontaneous or deliberate, and religious associations exhibit both types. Generally, the incipient stage lasts not much longer than a few months. If the object is worthy of attention and the association is sustainable, the next phase will be evident.

The efficient stage involves establishment of rules and protocols. Rules include a statement of purpose or mission, membership qualifications, sanctions, and communication with the public and the constituency of the association. The enthusiasm of the first generation of associates will lead to efficiency and enforcement of rules. The greatest test of the vitality and longevity of the voluntary association will be the transition from the leadership of the first to succeeding generations. The more urgent the objective is, whether due to the religious ideal or factors in the environment, the more likely will be the survival of the association.

The point at which the voluntary association moves from the efficient stage to the formal stage is often blurred. It is not necessarily evident from any loss of participation or lessening of enthusiasm. Rather, the formal stage is noted in retrospect by the association's preoccupation with form and structure, discipline, and informal protocols. Ritual replaces spontaneous expression, and members have a sense of routinization. The great principles and Christian

3. Hertzler, 79-82.

ideals of the association are no longer debated, but canonized. Leadership style during this stage becomes conservative, protective of powers, and isolated in an elite. Their leadership may become an end in itself. The financial assets of the association may grow in this stage, as well as the membership, through both astute enlistment and nurture. There may be a division between the active and passive participants.

The fourth stage, disorganization or disintegration, usually comes about slowly. Critique of the operation, unclear objectives, distant officers, and low participation are characteristic. Either death or reorganization will take place eventually at this stage. Among religious voluntary associations, there is often a high probability of resurrection or transformation into a new, more vital association. Rarely do religious associations die out completely.

Most social scientists believe that religious groups exhibit these life cycle stages as they move from sects to formal churches and denominations.[4] Since many churches and denominations did emerge first as voluntary associations of one kind or another, this is a valid application. The life-cycle hypothesis applied to long-term voluntary associations is even more germane to this discussion. To illustrate, a number of religious associations grew up in the early decades of the nineteenth century in the United States to foster the education of clergy. These associations thrived in the incipient and efficient stages by the ideals of Christian education and fund-raising. As the formal stage took shape, the need to increase assets and press the objectives and membership to the limits overrode the idealism of the earlier stages. Eventually, the institutional expressions of these associations became more important than the associations, and the professional managers of the colleges or seminaries supplanted the elected officers of the education societies. As the societies became antiques and, in some cases, statutorily extinct, institutions like

---

4. This was Max Weber's belief, and it is articulated in David Moberg as well. See Max Weber, *The Theory of Social and Economic Organization,* trans. A. M. Henderson and Talcott Parsons (New York: Oxford University Press, 1947), and David O. Moberg, *The Church as a Social Institution: The Sociology of American Religion* (Grand Rapids, Mich.: Baker Books, 1984), 118-22.

Colgate University, Acadia University, Bucknell University, and Gettysburg College resulted. In Britain a similar life cycle ensued in the case of many Nonconformist academies and their adjunct societies, notably Bristol Baptist College and Northern Baptist College. Similar life cycles of voluntary associations could be adduced in domestic and foreign missions and humanitarian societies.

As noted earlier, it is also possible to observe the life cycle of contemporary voluntary associations. The Lausanne Movement among international evangelicals is a fascinating case study. Founded in 1974, Lausanne is in the embryonic stages of structural development, and it gives evidence of the early stages of development.

At the invitation of American evangelist Billy Graham, 3,700 delegates and visitors met for over a week in Lausanne, Switzerland, in summer 1974 to discover new means for world evangelization. The congress, which evinced the incipient stage of associational development, produced a remarkable sense of unity among delegates of churches, individuals, and associations from 150 nations, 50 percent of whom were from "Two Thirds World" countries. The most important products of the congress were the "Lausanne Covenant" and the continuing Lausanne Committee. The Covenant was a three-thousand-word, fifteen-point statement of evangelical principles drafted by the British Anglican pastor John R. W. Stott (1921-).

An international continuing committee, formed shortly after the congress, signalled the emergence of the efficient stage of development. The purpose of the Lausanne Committee is "to further the evangelization of the world by building bridges of understanding and cooperation among Christian leaders everywhere. . . ." As a continuing body of well-reputationed clergy and laity from every continent (primarily Protestant), the Committee promotes evangelism, studies of biblical theology, prayer strategies, statistical and cultural data, religious liberty, and stewardship for evangelism. To give continual visibility to what the seventy-five-member committee desires to call a "movement" rather than a "power structure," persons of vision and experience are commissioned for specific tasks; regional international congresses are held; and special task groups are identified. Four working groups have defined the tasks of Lausanne: theology, strategy, intercession, and communications.

Sharply distinguishing itself from the "ecumenical movement," the Lausanne leadership stresses the integrity of the individual associations and church bodies that cooperate with it. In order to avoid structural predominance, the Committee is sustained by a small financial development office in Charlotte, North Carolina, led by Leighton Ford, formerly of the Graham organization. An equally simple programme function is supplied by a changing executive director, whose offices have been in Singapore; California; and Oxford, England. The executive committee meets biennially, and a second general international gathering, called Lausanne II, met at Manila in 1989.

The bonding element for the Lausanne Movement has been the Covenant. To participate in Lausanne activities, individuals, schools, churches, and other organizations are requested to sign the Covenant as a basis of common theological understanding and priorities.[5] Voluntary contributions are sought for a few common projects such as travel subsidies for currency-restricted delegates to attend meetings, newsletters, report books, and salaries for the development and programme offices. Voluntarism controls the ongoing programmes and regional projects; planning is done at delegates' expense; and the costs of meetings and services are borne by regional offerings and donations.

As the Lausanne Committee moves to embrace responsibilities for the evangelical community, not unlike the World Council of Churches for its constituency, its organizational maturing process proceeds toward the formal stage. Regional strategies for evangelization are calling for regular communications, the use of the Committee as the best clearinghouse of Christian information, and identification of institutions and networks that will shoulder ongoing leadership and tasks. From a recent list of critical objectives, it is also apparent that L.C.W.E. must enhance its development of financial resources, administration, and public relations — techniques learned as early as the seventeenth century among voluntary religious associations.

---

5. At Lausanne II in Manila in 1989 a second covenant was achieved that includes twenty-one affirmations and an essay on "the whole gospel." See "The Manila Manifesto: Calling the Whole Church to Take the Whole Gospel to the Whole World" (unpublished statement, July 1989).

A time gap has recently developed in the Lausanne life cycle. In the 1990s, the leadership has stepped back from the possibilities of formalism on the one hand and is testing the sustainability of professionalization on the other. Significantly, however, the Lausanne Committee continues to identify its primary mission as cooperation and its principal human resources as volunteers rather than staff paid from its own resources. Programmatically, L.C.W.E. at times becomes an international umbrella coalition for those churches, people, and fellowships in the evangelical theological traditions. In this role it competes more or less favourably with other evangelical bodies, notably the World Evangelical Fellowship. Time will reveal whether Lausanne will evolve into a more formal organization with an institutional identity.

The importance of identifying the stages of the associational life cycle is seen in the linkages of historical societies with contemporary associations. Moreover, if the voluntary impulse is a worthwhile dynamic of vital Christianity, its transformation into associations is of paramount importance to the leadership of the associations and those who are concerned with various forms of Christian renewal.[6]

II. External Patterns of Voluntary Associations

The history of the rise and success of Christian voluntary associations in Britain and North America over the past three centuries reveals a

6. Another recent example of the evolving life cycle of a religious voluntary association is the Association of Vineyard Churches, founded by John Wimber in 1986. The fellowship began as a prayer group in Anaheim, California, in 1977, and early in its history became a loose collection of charismatic fellowships devoted to recovering the "signs and wonders" of the New Testament churches. Recently, the Association has hired an "international coordinator" who has "withdrawn endorsement" from an errant member fellowship. See "Copy of a Letter to International Vineyard Pastors from Bob Fulton, International Coordinator, AVC," dated 13 December 1995, and other correspondence in the author's files relating to the Toronto Airport Blessing. For a Canadian assessment of the Vineyard phenomenon, see Norman J. Backhouse, "Signs and Wonders: Distinguishing the Baby from the Bathwater," in *Prairie Overcomer* (November 1987): 14-17.

number of important functions and results. There are four demonstrable patterns of voluntary associations in the combined transatlantic heritage: new directions, proliferation of an idea, increased cooperation, and critique. A functional historical analysis follows.

A. *Evolution Produces a New Direction*

A prominent example of how one voluntary association can breed a new generation of related activity lies in the heritage of the English Baptist Missionary Society. Formed in 1792 (see Chapter Three) by a legendary thirteen participants who gave a little over thirteen pounds sterling to the cause of evangelizing the heathen, the "Particular Baptist Missionary Society for Propagating the Gospel Among the Heathen" became a voluntaristic paradigm within the transatlantic Baptist community for what came to be known as the "society" method of Baptist missions. The dependence of the B.M.S. on earlier models has been demonstrated elsewhere. Its impact upon later Baptistic strategies was remarkable also.

1. *The Impact of the Baptist Missionary Society*

The impact of the Baptist Missionary Society upon theologically Calvinistic Baptist life in England was immediate. In order to raise funds for the William Carey mission planned for India, Andrew Fuller, Samuel Pearce (1746-1799), and John Ryland (1753-1825) travelled widely to establish a base of support for the Society. As the interest in global evangelism spread among the congregations, church leaders began to call for evangelism and renewal in England. John Fawcett (1740-1817) in Yorkshire was typical. At Hebden Bridge, a small church in the mining region, he advocated the establishment of an academy at Horton that would train leaders in the Northampton tradition. The first principal of that school, William Steadman (1764-1837), was the genius of a new system of education in the North, whereby student pastors were sent out among the associations to start new churches. Steadman was the driving force behind the Itinerant Society (later Home Mission Society) founded

91

in 1809. Historians have traced the revival among the Particular Baptist churches to virtually every part of England and Wales from "Fullerism" and the creation of the Baptist Missionary Society.

Indirectly related to the Baptist preoccupation with foreign missions were also several cognate enterprises facilitated by the society method. One of the leading voluntarist organizers in the era was Joseph Ivimey (1773-1834), who was active in the formation of the Baptist Itinerant Society and the Baptist Irish Society (1813). Spurred on by his work with the B.M.S., Ivimey proposed in 1811 the establishment of a union of all Baptists, essentially for voluntary service, which was the root of the denomination's structural development in Great Britain. Ivimey collected hundreds of pounds sterling for overseas missions through the channel of the Union meetings in London. One historian has thus characterized the Mission Society as a magnet upon the Baptist churches, drawing them together as never before in a common purpose with renewed life.

2. Baptist Societies in the United States

The impact of Baptist Missionary Society voluntarism was felt in the United States as well. William Staughton (1770-1829), who was among those present at the formation of the B.M.S., emigrated to the United States in the early nineteenth century and took with him the society principle of organization. Within a few short years, Staughton had organized an education society for Philadelphia Baptists, and he was proactive in raising the possibility of an American missionary society. When the opportunity arrived in 1813 to consolidate pro-missionary forces across the eastern states into a national voluntary association, Staughton was chosen the voluntary corresponding secretary of the General Baptist Missionary Convention. He obviously had much to do with the style of that organization.

Luther Rice (1783-1836), another American Baptist devotee of the society principle, embellished the foreign missionary idea to include education and publication, both of which strengthened the missionary enterprise in Rice's thinking. Yet another Baptist voluntarist was John Mason Peck (1789-1857), who built the domestic missionary society idea upon the model forged for the foreign mission body. In the 1840-1860 period, American Baptists further exploited the concept by forming the American Indian Mission Association (1842), the American Baptist Free Mission Society (1843, based on antimasonry and opposition to centralized organizations), and the Boston Baptist Bethel Society (1845). Later in the late 1870s, Baptist women again used the society principle to create voluntary associations for missionary purposes, ensuring that their associations were completely under female control.[7]

The Baptist voluntarist impulse in missions did not end with the nineteenth century. Following severe theological tensions in the opening decades of the twentieth century, American Baptists witnessed new waves of voluntarism that expanded the overseas witness. In 1927, the Association of Baptists for World Evangelism was formed in light of theologically fundamentalist demands in the Northern Baptist Convention. Later, in 1943, the Conservative Baptist Foreign Mission Society was created because of widespread antipathy to a theologically inclusive appointment policy, also in the Northern Baptist Convention. Among Baptists in the American South, the Premillennial Baptist Missionary Fellowship began in 1933, to be followed by the Baptist Missionary Association of America, formed by fundamentalist Baptists in 1950.

3. Baptist Societies in the Canadian Baptist Context

Canadian Baptists, too, eventually expressed high interest in the paradigm of the English Baptist Missionary Society. In 1827, the *Baptist Missionary Magazine of Nova Scotia and New Brunswick* featured inaugural pieces on William Ward and the Carey Mission in Calcutta. In volume one, number one, of the *Canada Baptist Magazine* (1837), there was a full treatment of William Carey and the Society's mission. The first Canadian Baptist voluntary association was the Nova Scotia

---

7. Among the associations formed were women's home and foreign mission societies in the east and west and two Freewill Baptist ladies' societies. For the list, see William H. Brackney, *Christian Voluntarism in Britain and North America: A Bibliography and Critical Assessment* (Westport, Conn.: Greenwood Press, 1995), 264-65.

Baptist Missionary Society, formed in 1815. Twenty-eight more voluntary associations followed in missionary work and education before the end of the century. Many of the Canadian Baptist voluntary associations languished and were short-lived, owing to intense antagonism between immigrant groups or denominational polity disputes. Still others competed between regions.

4. Voluntarism and Baptist Denominational Identity

One of the most remarkable evidences of voluntarism in the wake of the B.M.S. achievement is the transformation of Baptist denominational work. At the end of the eighteenth century, denominations were defined by a collection of churches holding to a common confession or heritage, as for instance the Baptists and Mennonites, respectively. When, however, the voluntary societies emerged as part of the same constituency and support network, leaders were quick to propose integration of the regular confessional bodies (associations, yearly meetings, synods, etc.) with the attractive and aggressive societies. The end result was that the confessional bodies came to legitimate the efforts of the societies, the societies became accountable through reports and publications to the associations, and so on. Gradually, through a series of common annual meetings and interlocking boards of trustees or directors, the society tradition was fused with the confessional bodies into a unified denominational identity and structure. For many Baptists, the societies became the "program agencies" of the denominations. From 1817 through the 1860s, this occurred in the coalition of the Baptist Union of Great Britain and Ireland, a product of General and Particular Baptist roots plus the results of the Irish missionary society's work. In the United States, the evolution of the original cooperating societies of northern Baptists to the Northern Baptist Convention and later the American Baptist Churches from 1907 through 1972 again illustrates the formation of a denominational consciousness from voluntary organizational roots. Worth noting in both of these examples is that fund-raising and nurture of the constituency were dramatically enhanced in the names of the objects of the voluntary societies.

94

B. Voluntarism Has Led to Proliferation of an Idea

Another important example of the evolutionary pattern of Christian voluntarism is found in the translation, publication, and distribution of Scripture. It became obvious to early missionaries in the wake of William Carey's missionary labours that Christian thought and culture were most effectively expressed from the Bible and most easily communicated in the indigenous languages. Translation of Scriptures were often a by-product of linguistic training for the missionaries themselves. The first European and North American missionaries all concentrated on translation efforts in their initial years in India, Africa, and China. The principal problem for missionary/translators came to be providing for copies and editions of what they produced, plus other literary tools such as dictionaries and commentaries. The denominational mission bodies that sent abroad the missionary personnel were not sufficiently endowed to sponsor the necessary publication work.

1. The Origins of Bible Societies

The first Bibles printed for wide distribution in the English language were produced by the S.P.C.K. The need for Welsh-language Scriptures led to pressure on this organization, but the Society only partially met the demand. For a time, the interdenominational Religious Tract Society (1799) produced Scripture portions. Eventually, through a series of fortuitous associations in 1802, a coterie of merchants and ministers from England and Wales covenanted with several friends in the Religious Tract Society to form a "Society for Promoting a More Extensive Circulation of the Holy Scriptures at Home and Abroad." The historian of the organization suggested that at first there was "doubt and sectarian prejudice," but the leaders pressed ahead with their idea.

In typical British voluntary fashion, a meeting of interested persons was called at the London Tavern in February 1804 and the Society "with too long a title" became simply the British and Foreign Bible Society, with three hundred persons involved from among Lutherans, Anglicans, Quakers, and a host of other denominations.

Three secretaries were chosen to represent broadly the constituency, and the Society had a single object: "to encourage the wider circulation of the Holy Scriptures, without note or comment." An executive committee of Anglicans and Nonconformists in equal numbers was chosen, and the first years of the Society were marked by an unusual catholicity of spirit. Unlike the U.S. "voluntary board tradition," the committee actually engaged in administrative work, which at times proved cumbersome. Indeed, given its usefulness to several other bodies involved in overseas work, the British and Foreign Bible Society soon claimed working alliances with the London Missionary Society, the Church Missionary Society, and the Sunday School Union. Targeting India, China, the South Seas, Canada, and Europe, within a dozen years the Society produced 1.6 million copies of the Scriptures.

Among the most important outgrowths of the formation of the British and Foreign Bible Society was its influence upon the foundation of similar voluntary bodies and the transformation of religious culture in Britain. Bible societies grew up in Edinburgh, in various parts of Europe, and especially for seamen during the Napoleonic Wars. Many of these were auxiliaries to the parent body, raising funds and specifying projects of interest to a local chapter that could be included in the larger work. (In 1812, for example, the Southwark Auxiliary in London employed 650 agents.) Even more importantly, one British historian believes, the Bible Society created a "serious" moral and religious public that opened the door for a widespread multiclass Victorian benevolence.[8] It was a model for many other efforts and was the primary paradigm in its own field of endeavour.

The Bible Society idea caught on in the United States as well. Missionaries for the American Board of Commissioners for Foreign Missions noted its success and usefulness in the British context and called for an American counterpart. Hostilities during the Napoleonic Wars between the British Empire and the United States suggested that American voluntarism would mature on its own. In 1816, an

8. Ford K. Brown, *Fathers of the Victorians: The Age of Wilberforce* (Cambridge: University Press, 1961).

American Bible Society was formed in New York City from among the major denominational groups and state Bible societies to serve the needs of the American missionary communities and the overseas bodies to whom they ministered. Under leaders like Archibald Maclay (1776-1860), a Scottish immigrant to the United States, and Elias Boudinot (1740-1821), the American counterpart to the British Bible Society movement sponsored translations first for native Americans and Burmese peoples. Primary in support were Methodists and Baptists. For several decades, cooperation for the American Bible Society was congenial and multidenominational.

Sectarian difficulties emerged for some groups. A group of clergy, led by New York City Baptist pastors, desired that the translations sponsored by the American Bible Society should reflect the literal reading of the New Testament Greek for the word *baptizo*. Thus "baptize" should be rendered "immerse." Obviously helpful to the Baptist position, this became a sore point for other denominations who did not practise immersion. Ultimately, the Baptists were displeased with the Bible Society board's decision, and they formed a new voluntary organization called the American and Foreign Bible Society in 1837. This short-lived body divided again, and a successor group, the American Bible Union, sponsored an edition of the Bible with the Baptist nuances in 1866. Ultimately the edition won few adherents and the Bible Union succumbed, leaving Baptist interests restored to the mainstream American Bible Society. With all of the internal dissensions, the American Bible Society managed to produce 1.9 million Scripture portions in its first twenty years of work. Its receipts averaged $60,000 annually for the same period.

In Canada, the Bible society movement took a bit different course. The first "foreign" translation made for the British and Foreign Bible Society was in fact for the Mohawk Nation in Upper Canada, and subsequently English Bibles were distributed in Nova Scotia in 1807. A branch society was formed in Nova Scotia in 1807, from which several auxiliaries to the British and Foreign Bible Society in Canada were connected. Eventually, in 1904, the centenary year of the B.F.B.S., a Canadian Bible Society, which continued to relate its work to the British body, was formed. True to the original paradigm, the charter for the organization spoke of its identity as "a voluntary society," by which it meant that the work was funded by voluntary gifts and administered by a voluntary board of directors. Eventually, the Canadian Bible Society sought an independent status from the British, until it joined forces in the 1940s with the United Bible Societies, an international federation of related voluntary groups. In its first decade of independent work, the Canadian Bible Society furnished over fifty million pieces of Scripture in many different tongues. A recent survey demonstrated that the Canadian Bible Society had evolved into a "not-for-profit" corporation with an administrative staff of eighty-one, an annual budget expenditure of over $12 million, an endowment of over $20 million, and hundreds of volunteer workers. Through the establishment of its effective alliances with major religious structures, the Bible Society has itself become a part of the dominant religious culture in the United States, Canada, and Great Britain.

2. Expanding the Idea

In addition to the mainstream Bible society movement, other associations emerged to meet the need for the Christian Scriptures. Each was based upon the principle originally expressed in the British and Foreign Bible Society.

At the turn of the twentieth century, two forward-looking organizations began in the United States and broadened to have international impacts. In 1898, two businessmen travelling together, John Nicholson and Samuel Hill, formed an Association for Christian Travellers. Following a lead from a similar British association, Nicholson came up with the idea to place wholesome reading materials, specifically the Bible, in hotels. In 1908, what was renamed the "Gideons" adopted the goal of placing the Scriptures in every hotel room in the United States. What distinguished the Gideons from the mainstream Bible society movement was their doctrinal statement that affirmed inerrancy, their placement of notes in each copy of the Bible they distributed, and their sole use of the King James Version.[9]

9. Phyllis Thompson, *The Gideons: The Story of the Gideons International in the British Isles* (London: Hodder and Stoughton, 1984), 2-29.

Organizationally, the Gideons developed first a North American network of voluntary "bands" of businessmen and professionals to support their mission. In 1947, following World War II, an international Extension Committee was formed and the American Gideons launched a plan to develop chapters in every country open to them. While support for the work is coordinated by an office staff, the heart of the Gideons is the thousands of volunteers who distribute the Scriptures and raise funds. Of primary importance to the Gideons is a strong relationship with local congregations, where Gideons take up a voluntary offering following a Sunday worship service devoted to their cause.

Influenced by the revival movement in England and North America, evangelistic efforts using Scripture portions led to the founding of the Pocket Testament League. In response to a children's need in England, evangelists Charles Alexander (1867-1920) and J. Wilbur Chapman (1859-1918) launched a worldwide organization in 1908 to distribute Scripture in convenient-sized editions as evangelism was conducted. Those involved in the movement were encouraged to carry the Bible with them and to engage in a programme of daily Bible reading. Based in the United States, the League maintains a small central professional staff and volunteers for distribution of the Scriptures. Representatives of the League visit local churches to interpret the ministry and collect offerings.

A third Bible-oriented association was the result of two colporters, L. L. Legters and W. Cameron Townshend (1896-1982). Townshend had been a colporter for the Bible House of Los Angeles in Latin America in 1917 and observed the translation need of the tribes on that continent. In 1934, he attended the Keswick Convention and received support for a new translation mission. Originally the support was channelled through the Pioneer Mission of Philadelphia, Pennsylvania. In 1934, Wycliffe Bible Translators Inc. was founded to "put the Word of God into all the tribal languages of the world that did not yet have the Scriptures." In recent years, Wycliffe Bible Translators has become one of the major parachurch associations in the evangelical world.

As of 1990 there were over twenty-five voluntary associations involved in Bible publication and distribution in the United States.

The proliferation of Scripture publication, then, illustrates vividly the evolution of voluntary means within a single enterprise.

C. The Voluntary Impulse in Ecumenical Relations

Ecumenical relationships and related activities have a long history in the life of the church. Generally, they are of two kinds: The majority involve arrangements of a formal nature between churches, which are negotiated and implemented officially by representatives of the cooperating churches. A second class, which will be examined here, is entirely voluntary.

1. The Evangelical Alliance

The formation of the Evangelical Alliance in August 1846 (mentioned earlier) provided a fountainhead of voluntary Christian cooperation. The ideal of the promoters of the Alliance was a union of individual Christians belonging to different churches — an experiment in Christian cooperation for the sake of combating "Popery, Puseyism, and Plymouth Brethrenism." Those invited were of the "voluntary system" and included over twelve thousand delegates to the official proceedings. The actual outgrowths of the Alliance meetings were a renewal of concerted prayer for Christian unity, increased information gathering about Christian endeavour, a defence of religious liberty, and a renewed interest in world missions. While it lacked a permanent paid staff, a forward-reaching programme, and consistent support from churches, the Alliance did create an entirely new climate of ecumenism among Protestant Christians. As ecumenical historian Ruth Rouse has pointed out, the Alliance gave great impetus to world mission. It expressed a new form of unity among diverse Christians and strengthened the whole principle of voluntary associations of Christians.[10] In direct linear progression from the Evan-

10. J. B. A. Kessler, *A Study of the Evangelical Alliance in Great Britain* (Goes: Oosterbaan and Cointre, 1968); David M. Howard, *The Dream That Would Not Die: The Birth and Growth of the World Evangelical Fellowship, 1846-1986* (Exeter: Pater-

gelical Alliance were the Student Volunteer Movement (1868), the World's Parliament of Religions (1893), and the International Missionary Council (1910). Indirectly through the International Missionary Council, the World Council of Churches (1948) also stands partly in this tradition.

2. The World Council of Churches

The World Council of Churches and its predecessors have been an indirect catalyst for voluntary evangelical ecumenism. While the Council itself has had a stormy history of constituency relationships, it has also indirectly prompted the voluntary association of other Christians for similar purposes. During the same period that a world council was under discussion from 1925 to 1948, numerous national bodies on the same model were taking shape with similar agendas. The Federal Council of Churches of Christ in the U.S. was a pioneer association in 1913; a British Council was approved by eleven denominations in 1942; a similar body was created in Canada in 1944. These councils often presaged the structural forum of the later World Council. Other cross-confessional cooperation and fellowships were also established on different bases. Of major importance of this latter type were the National Association of Evangelicals, founded in 1964 in the United States by a coalition of conservative and independent Evangelicals, and the Evangelical Fellowship of Canada (an outgrowth in 1964 of the U.S. movement), founded by two Pentecostal pastors from Toronto. Both of these groups reflected the need for "Evangelical" cooperation, yet neither proposed to interfere with the affairs of any denomination per se. Individual memberships and churches contribute to these organizations with annual conferences for fellowship and scholarly exchanges constituting the thrust of the voluntarism. At the international level, the World Association of

---

noster Press, 1986); John Wolffe, "The Evangelical Alliance in the 1840s: An Attempt to Institutionalize Christian Unity," in *Voluntary Religion,* ed. W. J. Sheils and Diana Wood (Oxford: Basil Blackwell, 1986); Ruth M. Rouse and Stephen Neill, eds., *A History of the Ecumenical Movement* (Geneva: World Council of Churches, 1986), 320.

Evangelicals (founded in 1961) provides periodic fellowship for the national groups. As the individual denominations have been unable or unwilling to seek closer cooperation in any organic sense through the concilliar vehicle, confessional voluntarism has provided an effective vehicle for experimentation and fellowship.

What the voluntary impulse toward ecumenical relationships demonstrates most vividly is the tendency of like-minded congregations or religious groups to seek fellowship and cooperation with each other, a premise that is basic to the voluntary principle. It is not the relational issue of "ecumenism" that is at stake, but the determination of which ecumenical relationship a voluntary body may embrace.

D. Voluntarism Provides a Vehicle for Critique

One of the most significant patterns of voluntarism that illustrates this organizational evolution is critique: the capability to assess weakness and inadequacies in existing institutions and provide an alternative. In the seventeenth-century English context, this was labelled "dissent." For much of the seventeenth century, dissenting groups were uncertain of their status, largely due to the hostile political environment in England until Toleration. As the dissenting traditions organized more formally and became routine in their behaviour, adopting permanent structures and paid ministers and staff, a new set of religious denominations was born. The growth of English sectarianism in the eighteenth century, then, as the logical conclusion of dissent, is a model for understanding a long-term cycle of voluntarism.

Not all religious dissent has had a voluntary quality about it. The confessional churches of the Reformation, for instance, provided a variegated critique of Roman Catholicism, yet Catholicism was frequently replaced with a parish structure or episcopacy and distinct paracongregational lines of authority and accountability. The *collegia pietatis* in the Pietist tradition critiqued a lethargic religious circumstance by a call for renewal within the same structures and lines of authority. Like other categories of "older" English Dissent, Methodism in the eighteenth century was at first a voluntary renewal tradition within the Church of England. Then it grew into a hierarchical connectional church institution, remarkably akin to its parent body.

The larger Methodist heritage illustrates the voluntary critique pattern. The history of the "come-outer" traditions in the United States and Canada shows how critique within the Methodist churches led to new organizations and movements. In three successive waves of concern, the main body of episcopal Methodists absorbed severe critique over structural, moral, and ethical issues.

In 1792, a movement arose in the American Methodist Episcopal General Conference over ministerial rights and lay representation at conference sessions. Led by James O'Kelly (1757-1826) of Virginia in the 1790s and William S. Stockton (1808-1868) of New Jersey in the 1830s, this critique eventually became the formal separation known as the Methodist Protestant Church. "Democratic Methodism," as it came to be called, eventually returned to a more lay-representative Methodism in the union of 1939.

A second point of difficulty for a vocal regional minority was the relative indifference to slavery exhibited in the General Conferences, beginning in 1832. Preachers like Orange Scott (1800-1847), Luther Lee (1800-1889), and Lucius Matlack (fl. 1840-1870) led the charge for abolition of slavery. After repeated defeats in the General Conferences, Lee and his cohorts organized the Wesleyan Methodist Connection, a voluntary body of antislavery activists. The Connection provided a forum of conscience on a variety of social concerns, including women's rights and opposition to secret societies, from 1843 to the War Between the States. After the Civil War and Emancipation, interest among the original leaders for a separate Methodist body waned and many returned to the Methodist Episcopal Church. However, advocates of holiness theology in the Allegheny (Pennsylvania) Conference revived antagonism to secret societies and pursued the themes of perfectionistic theology, thus making the Wesleyan Methodists a permanent reform feature of American Methodism.[11]

11. Ira F. MacLeister, *History of the Wesleyan Methodist Church of America* (Syracuse, N.Y.: Wesley Press, 1951), 88.

Similar to the movement that became Wesleyan Methodism, a third form of critique among American Methodists was theological and ethical. From the 1830s, perfectionist tendencies had made great inroads among rural Methodists. Evangelist Phoebe Palmer (1807-1874) was a prime mover of "entire" or "crisis" sanctification, by which was meant a second work of grace manifested in holiness of life toward God. A young Methodist pastor, Benjamin T. Roberts (1823-1893), experienced sanctification while at a camp meeting with Mrs. Palmer in 1850 and took up the theme in the Lockport and Genesee (New York) Conferences. Several Methodist Episcopal congregations soon coalesced around camp-meeting revivalism, perfectionistic theology (actually antagonism to worldliness), lay representation, and abhorrence of secret societies. Borne along by lay interests, the movement grew in opposition to "New School" or "liberal" Methodism. In 1860, Roberts and others organized formally the "Free Methodist Church."[12]

All three of these "come-outer" voluntary critiques within the Methodist tradition in the United States and Canada led to permanent organizations that spread their networks across North America. The cycle of critique was completed for the Methodist Protestants who rejoined the Methodist Episcopals (North and South) in 1939, for the Wesleyan Methodists in 1872 when they defined themselves as a church, and for the Free Methodists in 1915. Both of these latter groups considered merger in the late 1960s, as they had come to be so close in congregational proximity and theological identity.[13]

12. Leslie Marston, *From Age to Age: A Living Witness* (Winona Lake, Ind.: Light and Life Press, 1960), 249-71.

13. Actually several branches of "come-outer" Methodism considered union as early as 1860. This union movement would have rapidly institutionalized the sects if it had been realized. See William H. Brackney, "Church Union in the Come-outer Tradition: Wesleyan Methodists and Methodist Protestants, 1858-1867," *Methodist History* 24:2 (January 1986): 82-97.

Summary

The application of social science methods to the study of voluntary societies produces unique insights into this important organizational phenomenon. Internal patterns are observable as part of a life cycle; this can be seen in historical development as well as in the contemporary religious landscape. The Lausanne Movement provides a fascinating ongoing case study. Further, a functional analysis of voluntary associations demonstrates the important contributions these associations have made to the development of adequate and appropriate forms for Christian endeavour. Among the noteworthy contributions are renewal, cooperation, growth, and critique.

PART II

PRAXIS

CHAPTER SIX

How Religious Voluntary Organizations Function

Having surveyed the biblical, theological, and historical roots of Christian voluntarism, it is now appropriate to turn to a considera-tion of the most enduring manifestation of the voluntary impulse, the voluntary religious association. Voluntary religious associations have transformed Christian work in Britain and North America and continue to do so in the form of parachurch organizations in the twentieth century. Admittedly, until recently when major shifts have been observed in North American religious culture, little attention has been paid to this organizational phenomenon. Included in this discussion will be a consideration of the pathologies of voluntary associations and patterns of organizational disintegration.

I. The Formation of Associations

Voluntary associations begin with a cluster of persons interested in accomplishing a purpose or being identified in a particular way. As shown in Chapter Five, this may be in response to a perceived need or a new endeavour. At the informal stage of development, the persons may meet infrequently and be unclear about the focus of the association. Such organizations may not last long in the informal stage. For religious associations, the informal stage can involve an enthusiastic response to a catalytic event, like an awakening experience, or a response to the appeal of a charismatic leader's appeal.

When consensus has been reached about the object of the association, its urgency, and the need for a long-term association, more formal steps in organization take place. A constitution and bylaws may be written, the means for permanent financial support will be agreed upon, and, most importantly, leadership will emerge. Finally, the association will develop strategies for accomplishing its purpose and interpreting its identity. Various forms of the media will be especially useful to announce strategies to the constituency.

II. Voluntary Religious Associations

There are several ways to classify religious organizations, as legal, ecclesiastical corporations (defined by either canon or civil law), unions, conventions, conferences, synods, presbyteries, missions, stakes, associations, or meetings. Such terms are derived from churchly or denominational nomenclature. Broadly speaking, a "church" as a social institution is defined as "an autonomous corporate institution hierarchically organized and served by a professional priesthood."[1] To understand the "types" of church institutions, historical social scientists employ several paradigms, some of which have important implications for an analysis of religious associations.[2] In recognition that in North America, a free, religiously pluralistic society prevails and that all church

---

1. Bryan R. Wilson, "Religious Organizations," in David L. Sills, ed., *International Encyclopedia of the Social Sciences,* vol. 13 (New York: Macmillan, 1968), 434.

2. These include "communal/associational": Gerhard Lenski, *The Religious Factor: A Sociological Study of Religion's Impact on Politics, Economics, and Family Life* (New York: Doubleday, 1961), 10-22; "prime beneficiary": Peter M. Blau and W. Richard Scott, *Formal Organizations: A Comparative Approach* (San Francisco: Chandler, 1962), 42-57; "authority/domination": Max Weber, *The Protestant Ethic and the Spirit of Capitalism* (New York: Charles Scribner's Sons, 1930); "corporate/federated": William A. Glaser and David L. Sills, eds., *The Government of Associations: Selections from the Behavioral Sciences* (Totawa, N.J.: The Bedminster Press, 1966), 22; "compliance structure": Amitai Etzioni, *Modern Organizations* (Englewood Cliffs, N.J.: Prentice Hall, 1964), 59-60.

bodies operate to some degree as voluntary associations,[3] the coercive organizational elements should be separated from the voluntary. While no "types" are perfect, a simple structural typology with the familiar three "ideal" types or categories — "episcopal," "presbyterial," and "congregational" — has much to commend its utility.[4] Generally speaking, the episcopal and presbyterial types are institutional and the congregational may be either institutional or voluntary or evolving from one to the other. If in fact the organization is legitimated by rules governing its operation, if its participants are professional, if it has endured to a formal structure, and if it affects a significant population, it may be classified as a microsocial unit or "institution."

Among the major examples of church institutions of the episcopal type are the Roman Catholic Church, the Episcopal (Anglican) Church, and the Methodist Churches. In 1917 the Roman Catholic Church defined categories within "Catholic Action" of holy offices, sacred orders, secular third orders, confraternities, and pious unions. Each of the categories is defined by canon law and accountable to the church, even those that display certain voluntary behaviours.[5] The United Methodist Church in the United States has long defined itself as a "church" with several levels of delegated authority in national, regional, and local conferences. Methodists have made provision in their conference structures for noninstitutional forms, but accountability still lies with the institution.[6] In

3. Gibson Winter, *The New Creation as Metropolis* (New York: Macmillan, 1963), 72ff.

4. For a fuller explanation of this typology and its limitations, see Richard D. Knudten, ed., *The Sociology of Religion: An Anthology* (New York: Appleton Century Crofts, 1967), 121-22.

5. T. L. Bowscaren, S.J., and A. G. Ellis, S.J., *Canon Law: A Text and Commentary* (Milwaukee, Wis.: Bruce Publishing Co., 1946), 360ff.

6. The Methodist Episcopal Church was constituted institutionally in 1784 at the Christmas Conference by Francis Asbury, its first bishop. Later, in 1939, the Methodist Church brought together three major strands of American Methodists into a single corporate entity. Finally, in 1966-1968, a merger blended the former Evangelical United Brethren Church with the mainstream of Methodism to form The United Methodist Church. See *The Book of Discipline of The United Methodist Church* (Nashville, Tenn.: The United Methodist Publishing House, 1976), 19-22.

the presbyterial type are the Presbyterian bodies, Lutherans, the Reformed Churches, and several smaller groups in the black traditions. More of the congregational type are the Baptists, Congregationalists, Independents, and many smaller sects. Illustrative of the interplay between the coercive and the voluntary elements, and the evolutionary tendencies, the highly decentralized American Baptist Churches in the U.S.A. has a governing accountability that is formalized through a series of covenants and shared expectations and funds, but still retains vestiges of nineteenth-century voluntary societies.[7]

As implied above, most religious organizations as institutions are coercive to one degree or another. The majority of church organizations from the beginning of the modern era have maintained well-defined structures of authority with elaborate theological rationales. Membership may be defined by geographical location, initiatory rite, or political decision. Decision making may be restricted to an elite, for instance, the ordained clergy or elected presbyters. This was especially true of Old World ecclesiastical systems like the Roman Catholic Church, the Lutheran Churches, and the Reformed Churches, even when transplanted to the New World. Finally, many church bodies rely upon tithes, membership assessments, or invested funds to achieve their purposes. Most of these characteristics would be lacking or secondary in voluntary associations; thus churches may be considered social institutions in their own right.

Since the mid-nineteenth century, institutional church structures in Britain and North America carry on most of the functions that earlier independent societies managed. A church body may conduct mission through its assignment of clergy to that task. A bishop may authorize an educational institution and provide church funds to support it. Decisions are made about various programmes of the church by its managers, that is, "ecclesiocrats" or delegated committees of assignment. Such management systems are clergy-

---

7. For an analysis of this group, see Paul M. Harrison, *Authority and Power in the Free Church Tradition* (Carbondale, Ill.: Southern Illinois University Press, 1959).

dominant and supported by the tradition of theological education and professional management associations.[8]

A second type of organization, in contrast with religious institutions, is noncoercive, less structured, voluntary in style, and essentially leisure-time in engagement. This type of organization may be classified as "voluntary associations." To underscore an earlier definition, organizational sociologists define voluntary associations as "all non-state common purpose organizations with voluntary memberships."[9] Further, most would assert that, to be a valid "voluntary" association, it must have a common purpose not related to the economic activities of the members, and voluntary members must constitute a majority of the participants. If the common or main purpose is religious, that is, if religious values or beliefs are the reason for the association's existence or provide the rationale for the common purpose, then the group may be classified as a religious voluntary association. The importance of religious voluntary associations cannot be overstated, as Ross Scherer suggests: "religious associations were one of the earliest forms of association in history and innovations in religious organization have been formative. . . ."[10]

Membership in a voluntary association for religious purposes is a critical determinant. To be effective, membership must be carefully defined. For instance, it cannot include all the individuals characterized by its purpose, nor necessarily those who are remotely in sympathy. That would be entirely coercive on the one hand and ineffective on the other. Rather, a voluntary association consists of those persons who make a conscious decision both to identify with the association's purpose and to support the object actively. The

8. Through the Association of Theological Schools in the United States and Canada, expectations and standards are set for leadership across confessional lines and theological traditions. To maintain the profiles of various categories of leaders, professional associations of chief executive officers, financial officers, fund-raisers, archivists, and librarians (to mention just a few) have emerged in North America.

9. David L. Sills, "Voluntary Associations — Sociological Aspects," in *International Dictionary of Social Science,* vol. 15 (New York: Macmillan, 1968), 363-78.

10. Ross P. Scherer, "The Church as a Formal Voluntary Association," in David H. Smith, *Voluntary Action Research: 1972* (Lexington, Mass.: Lexington Books, 1972), 81.

exclusive nature of certain types of religious associations may also be an important means of asserting social identity.[11]

The dynamics of participation in a religious voluntary association continue the principle of voluntarism at each level. Two kinds of participation are typical: participation in the decision making of the association is primary, and contribution of time, money, and goods, especially to religious associations, is a secondary kind of participation. Members are recruited voluntarily; decisions are usually made by democratic process to ensure the members that they do in fact participate; and leadership changes are also made by democratic process to avoid the perception that coercive means have replaced the voluntary nature of the association. In modern religious associations, a nominating process often carries the procedure for leadership identification. However, most associations still allow for nominations to be submitted from the voting membership at the time of the election. Here the influence of *Roberts' Rules of Order* or other procedural manuals has overridden a more purely democratic voluntary principle.[12]

The support of a voluntary association, or how members contribute to the object of the association, is a second important indicator of its voluntary nature. Purely voluntary associations subsist on the contributions of the membership. In Western Protestantism, strategies of contribution generate from the fifteenth-century idea of the church rooted in the Anabaptist tradition and the English Separatist groups, as well as the model of trading companies and social clubs. Early on, however, among the seventeenth-century missionary associations, such means of support proved inadequate, both because the objects of the association were far-reaching and because there evolved a need for consistent financial support. The vision of leadership was an important factor.

11. Illustrating this exclusivity in North America are the Conference on Faith and History, an evangelical scholars' association, and the Roger Williams Fellowship, a group of Baptists defined by their stance on religious liberty and personal freedom of thought.

12. Henry M. Robert, *Robert's Rules of Order* (New York: Jove Books, 1977), 21-22, 155-82; John G. Bourinot, *Bourinot's Rules of Order*, rev. J. Gordon Dubroy (Toronto: McClellan and Stewart, 1963), xi, 73-78.

By the turn of the eighteenth century among the early English voluntary societies, solicitation was added to membership support. Solicitation included new subcategories of membership (for those not involved in the decision making of the association), sales of materials, acceptance of bequests, and investment of funds held in trust. The New England Company used a variety of methods, including newspaper ads, mass distribution of tracts, and regional collectors.[13] Roman Catholic associations have also employed begging as a means of solicitation, and the Salvation Army would later develop a plan for random public collections.[14]

Some associations by the nineteenth century had developed such a need for elaborate business management that paid staff were employed in the work of management, investments, and solicitation. The British and Foreign Bible Society is an example of the transition from a purely voluntary association to a modified business institution.[15] However, great efforts have been made in this organization and its later affiliates to continue the voluntary management principle through a voluntary board and voluntary agencies.

Voluntary organizations have thrived on volunteer involvement. The greatest amount of energy in the life cycle of a voluntary organization is seen at its beginning stage, when participants are first engaged in its object. In order to continue to maintain that high level of enthusiasm for the object of the association, an elaborate accountability system and decision-making procedures have evolved. Typi-

13. William Kellaway, *The New England Company 1649-1776* (London: Longmans, Green & Co., 1961), 21-28; W. O. B. Allen and Edmund McClure, *Two Hundred Years: The History of the Society for Promoting Christian Knowledge 1698-1898* (New York: Burt Franklin, 1970), 136-37, 494-505.

14. On the Catholic practise of begging, see Charles Neely's article, "Begging," in Paul K. Meagher et al., eds., *Encyclopedic Dictionary of Religion*, vol. 1 (Philadelphia: Sisters of St. Joseph, 1979), 401-2. For the Salvation Army's tactics of solicitation in this regard, consult Robert Sandhall, *History of the Salvation Army, vol. 3, 1878-1886* (London: Thomas Nelson, 1950), 90, and Edward H. McKinley, *Marching to Glory: The History of the Salvation Army in the United States of America, 1880-1980* (San Francisco: Harper and Row, 1980), 60, 71.

15. The story of the evolution is told in William Canton, *A History of the British and Foreign Bible Society* (London: John Murray, 1904).

cally, an association holds an annual meeting of its membership. This "celebration," some historians believe, is the result of the evolution of ancient convivial feasts of social clubs and guild members. Greek and Roman societies held monthly banquets and stressed the fellowship nature of their associations, as did Italian, German, and English guild meetings.[16] The typical "event" included ritual (like prayer or singing or readings), eating, and reporting. In the English religious traditions, the meetings were held in coffeehouses and taverns. Generally, a significant personality was asked to address the membership on the merits of the association or project. These speeches most always resulted in an appeal for funds from the members present.[17]

The officers of an association are most visible at the annual meetings, presiding, reporting, and recording. Officers are typically elected at these meetings. From ancient practises among the Greeks and Romans, "archons," "magisters," treasurers, stewards, priests, and secretaries constituted the central offices. In later seventeenth-century English experience, officers like a president, secretary, treasurer, and steward formed a "court" for a typical association.

Following the annual meetings, ongoing interest must be sustained. For the broader constituency, reports are printed and distributed widely amongst both members and likely donors or membership prospects. Sermons and statistics in pamphlet form were the first literary evidences of many associations, and these appeared also in newspapers and periodicals.[18] It is noteworthy that many religious magazines in both the British and North American experiences owe their origins to voluntary associations that decided to nurture their constituencies by regular journalistic appeal.

16. Compare Samuel Dill, *Roman Society from Nero to Marcus Aurelius* (New York: Meridian Books, 1956), 279-83 with George H. Stevenson, "Roman Clubs," in *The Oxford Classical Dictionary,* ed. M. Cary et al. (Oxford: Clarendon Press, 1945), 205.

17. Allen and McClure, 126-29.

18. For an example of a sermon, see John Eliot, *Strength Out of Weakness, or a Glorious Manifestation of the Further Progress of the Gospel Among the Indians in New England* (London: M. Simmons, 1652). The collected data of the S.P.G. is found in "A Short Abstract of the Most Material Proceedings and Occurrences of the Society for the Propagation of the Gospel in Foreign Parts Between Feb. 1709/10 and Ditto 1710/11," which was attached to the annual sermon for 1711.

Symbolic leadership is also important to the vitality of a religious voluntary association. In the ancient world, clubs used the names of gods or great teachers. Catholic sodalities have used saints or the Blessed Virgin, and still others have symbolized leadership or sponsorship through the use of a family crest or coat-of-arms. The support of a prominent bishop or a leading businessperson or barrister as a "patron," indicated by his or her printed address or reported contribution, was a powerful incentive for others to support the association. Names like Daniel Williams (1643-1716), Henry Ashurst (1614-1680), Robert Boyle (1627-1691), Daniel Defoe (1691-1731), and the lords Archbishop of Canterbury were highly coveted supporters.[19] Anglicans had the advantage of occasionally enjoying the patronage of the royal household — Queen Anne (1665-1714) gave her princely munificence in 1703, and the use of her name helped to produce almost three thousand pounds sterling in 1711.[20] Such membership-nurturing practises began in Greece and Rome, persisted in English tradition with the New England Company and the Anglican societies at the beginning of the eighteenth century, and have continued to the twentieth-century associational experience.

For most, voluntary Christian service grows out of a love for Christ and a sincere desire for Christian service. This may be based upon a direct sense of serving Christ from a biblical paradigm (as with Francis of Assisi), such as caring for the sick or preaching an evangelistic sermon for a mission society or advocating justice when a biblical principle has been violated. Or, for some, the service may be mediated through the church where a person believes that faithful voluntary endeavour through the church fulfills the demand of the gospel for discipleship. This is true of the faithful Anglican who participated in a community food cupboard or the Baptist woman

19. The Presbyterian Fund, made possible by the Act of Toleration, sought to build a treasury to assist ministers and widows among the Presbyterians. Seven prominent clergy plus three times that many "gentlemen" and professionals made up the subscription list in 1692: "Minutes of the Board of the Presbyterian Fund," 1 July 1690–26 June 1693 (mss. in Dr. Williams Library), vol. 2, 2.

20. "An Account of the Society for the Propagation of the Gospel in Foreign Parts," 4 Feb. 1703 (broadside in Lambeth Palace Library); "Abstract of the Proceedings of the Society for the Propagation of the Gospel," 51.

who raised funds for the denominational missionary society. The importance of service for God, with Christ as an example, is an important ideal in the history of Christian voluntarism. Once set free to do good works, volunteers historically appear to be highly motivated to work for the sense of the approbation of Christ.

III. Why People Join a Religious Association

There is scant information on individual participation in voluntary associations. What does exist must be extrapolated from voluntary associations in general and from impressionistic observations. Studies of voluntary associations in general have shown that people join associations basically for four reasons: small-group interaction, identification with the object of the association, social identification, and theological identification. Each of these will be applied to the specific category of religious voluntary associations.

1. Small-Group Interaction

Small-group interaction has long been a desirable form of socialization, particularly in industrial societies. The family may provide sufficient necessary affirmations, identity, and correctives for children and adolescents. For many in an industrialized society, vocation leads to various forms of collective socialization, and people become part of various communities: a company, an assembly line, a union, a sales team, and the like. But persons may still wish to ease loneliness, learn a set of norms, or acquire specific information. Voluntary associations can thus become connecting links between the family and larger social institutions in the socialization process, as well as sources of great personal satisfaction. Such associations, believes one observer, provide individuality and personal caring — "a safe haven in a sea of bureaucracy."[21] Members of associations come to enjoy alternative "families" of interest with whom they interact. Role defi-

21. Robert Wuthnow, *Acts of Compassion: Caring for Others and Helping Ourselves* (Princeton, N.J.: Princeton University Press, 1991), 269.

nition, social experimentation, and recreation are also typical benefits produced by a voluntary association for its members.[22] There are hints that such factors as school experience, parental orientation, race, sex, the media, and geographical location affect the number and kind of associations in which people participate.[23]

The development of social and leadership skills for persons in Christian endeavour includes learning to communicate effectively, resolving conflict amicably, understanding political processes, working with practical economics, and observing role models. Beyond their purely personal benefits, religious associations also may confer a ceremonial recognition (e.g., ordination, installation) on the attainment of skills that are highly valued in the traditions of the religious community. Moreover, there may be overarching theological implications that involve the transcendent. This too increases the value of personal skills in a Christian community or enterprise.

2. Enhancement of Social Skills

Voluntary associations may improve social skills. Personality traits associated with outgoing attitudes, congeniality, and trust on the one hand, and dominance and assertiveness on the other, are factors relating to membership and participation. Because voluntarists are likely to be persons of higher intellectual capacity and breadth, there may be an expectation that skills and relationships will improve as a result of participation. By the volunteer nature of the association, a certain degree of equality of opportunity is therefore expected. If this is not practised, members may activate their voluntary option to drop out of the association and replace it with a more desirable

22. In a recent collection of fourteen narratives, Robert Wuthnow demonstrated the great variety of some of these associations: *"I Come Away Stronger": How Small Groups Are Shaping American Religion* (Grand Rapids, Mich.: Eerdmans, 1994). An older, useful study is Leon H. Levy, "Self-Help Groups — Types and Psychological Processes," in Herbert H. Blumberg et al., *Small Groups and Social Interaction* (New York: John Wiley & Sons, 1983), 227-37.

23. David Horton Smith and Richard D. Reddy, "An Overview of the Determinants of Individual Participation in Organized Voluntary Action," in David H. Smith, *Voluntary Action Research: 1972* (Lexington, Mass.: Lexington Books, 1972), 333.

association. Members will look for mutual respect of opinion, freedom of expression, and respect for leadership within the association. Members will typically look for an affirmation of their personal contribution to an association as a measure of their satisfaction or growth in the skills and/or experiences desired.

The small-group opportunity in most voluntary associations will produce tangible results in the socialization process for both individuals and the society. Members of an association will rotate leadership, and thus experiment with their own leadership skills as well as observe the roles of leadership in society. Skills like presiding over a meeting, record keeping, accounts management, correspondence with constituency, conflict resolution, and extensive socialization are typically included in the association experience. For persons in nonmanagerial vocational roles, the association may provide a primary experience and thus great satisfaction in socialization. For the society, a fresh cadre of leaders is thus created within voluntary associations.[24]

3. Social Identification

Social identification of a member is also an important factor. Writers like H. Richard Niebuhr (1894-1962) long ago observed the fundamental social bases of religious denominations,[25] and this same set of criteria helps to explain why some people join voluntary associations of a definite religious character. In nineteenth-century urban United States and Canada, for instance, Protestant Irish joined the Orange Lodge movement, while Catholic Irish joined the Hibernian Societies and the Knights of Columbus.[26] Likewise, largely rural

24. Nicholas Babchuk and John N. Edwards, "Voluntary Associations and the Integration Hypothesis," *Social Inquiry* 35 (1965): 149-62.

25. H. Richard Niebuhr, *The Social Sources of Denominationalism* (New York: Henry Holt, 1929), 26-28.

26. In Canada in particular, multicultural cultural pluralism has compelled significant numbers of people to join ethnically identifiable, religiously affiliated voluntary associations to maintain a certain social identity: Alan Frizzell and Elia Zureik, "Voluntary Participation: The Canadian Perspective," in David H. Smith, *Voluntary Action Research: 1974* (Lexington, Mass.: Lexington Books, 1974), 254-58.

Wesleyan Methodists have opposed secret societies such as the Freemasons, while predominantly urban episcopal Methodists joined the Free and Accepted Lodge in significant numbers. More recently, evangelical Christians have clustered around the quasi-recreational religious associations like the "Praise the Lord (PTL) Club" and other time-sharing vacation or theme center programmes. On the other hand, traditional mainstream denominationalists have tended to join outdoor or religious recreational groups at retreat centers or religious assembly or "Chautauqua" locations for golf, water sports, and spiritual/intellectual interaction.[27]

Identification with the object of the association is of primary socialization importance. The purpose of an association may actualize an individual's attitude or long-cherished goal. Associations can help supplement vocation and family as places and relationships where persons can realize significant self-fulfillment with others of like passion. Humanitarian associations with a religious basis, particularly supporting the care of disadvantaged persons, aid for the hungry, and human rights associations, illustrate this tendency.[28]

Voluntary associations can also reflect and enhance social status. Associations that allow for intermingling of social classes can be very attractive for persons in certain socioeconomic groups. Studies have shown that there is a positive correlation between socioeconomic status and the number of memberships one maintains in voluntary associations. Factors include stage in the life cycle, family size, occupational mobility, and family or lineage status.[29] This profile has been illustrated in religious groups like the Bible societies, Y.M.C.A. and Y.W.C.A., and among supporters of twentieth-century televangelists, where laypersons or representatives of the working class can

27. These denominational centers are located across the United States and include Chautauqua, New York; Green Lake, Wisconsin; Lake Junaluska, North Carolina; and Glorietta, New Mexico.

28. A large variety of typical associations for these purposes is listed in Carolyn A. Fischer and Carol A. Schwartz, eds., *The Encyclopedia of Associations, 1996,* vol. 1 (New York: Gale Research, 1996), 2459-75, and Linda Thurn, ed., *Encyclopedia of Associations: International Organizations,* part 1 (New York: Gale Research, 1996), 1567-1633.

29. Smith and Reddy, "Overview of Determinants," 332.

interact with managers, professionals, and socially prominent personalities who are involved in not only the fund-raising side of an association, but often also its primary object. The Full Gospel Businessmen's Fellowship International is an organization of quasi-charismatic Christian businesspeople who not only meet for regular fellowship and nurture across confessional lines, but also form a kind of local Christian commercial list.

Some voluntary participants may entertain career objectives that advance their social status, sharpen their sense of personal identity, or reduce their socialization to a fairly intimate group. Especially when this fails to happen, but also in the natural course of development, voluntary associations may help to achieve the same purposes. Sometimes the voluntary associations become more compelling than the vocational pursuits, as in the historic case of Anthony Ashley Cooper, seventh Earl of Shaftsbury (1801-1885), in the British Victorian era. Shaftsbury participated in almost forty different associations.[30] J. Howard Pew (1882-1971) of Philadelphia was a silent associate in numerous associations on the mid-twentieth-century American Evangelical scene.[31]

4. Religious Identification

Voluntary associations for religious purposes serve a direct purpose of religious identification for many people. While almost no data exist for this category of evaluation, it is obvious among persons with a heightened religious interest that involvement and participation in a religious act or association is fundamental to their religious affections. Religious altruism can be a motivating factor for participation among Christians. This can take the shape of receiving personal joy from service or identifying and assuming the suffering

---

30. The best work on this pivotal figure, which examines his evangelical theology also, is J. Wesley Bready, *Lord Shaftsbury* (New York: Frank Maurice, 1927).

31. For a synopsis of Pew's life see Mary Senholtz, *Faith and Freedom: The Journal of a Great American, J. Howard Pew* (Grove City, Pa.: Grove City College, 1975).

circumstances of others. Often, a church relationship will cover a wide area of experiences — worship, the sacraments/ordinances, administration, education, and service — but will provide only an ambivalent religious identity. It is increasingly evident that church institutions rationalize these activities to the extent that most church members are only spectators in the Christian experience. Even religious philanthropy only allows one to do something "for" someone else, rather than with someone else.

Religious voluntarism thus can provide an effective opportunity for collective religious altruism. To supplement their church membership, activist Christians may join associations that focus upon human need. Typically, this secondary kind of participation involves contributing money, time, or goods.[32] It may be exceedingly important to certain Christians to take literally the words of Christ to feed the hungry; thus one associates with a mission or relief agency. Still others may wish to adopt a less materialistic lifestyle and join a countercultural community like the Jesus People of the 1960s.[33] Still others may take the missionary imperative to themselves and participate in the work of an overseas organization by voluntary service or domestic support services. Most British and North American denominations and many religious voluntary associations provide for this type of voluntarist participation.

Another interesting type of religious identification is theological distinction. Some people join an association because it defines or sharpens their theological identity. Good examples of this religious function are the various forms of evangelical organizations like the Evangelical Theological Society, the Evangelical Fellowship of Canada, the National Association of Evangelicals (U.S.), the Wesleyan Theological Society, the Full Gospel Businessmen's Fellowship International, and the British Evangelical Alliance of the past century. A

32. This is the pattern found in North America: David Horton Smith and Burt R. Baldwin, "Voluntary Associations and Volunteering in the United States," in David H. Smith, *Voluntary Action Research: 1974* (Lexington, Mass.: Lexington Books, 1974), 289-91.

33. See the analysis in David DiSabatino, "The Jesus People Movement: Counterculture Revival and Evangelical Renewal" (unpublished M.T.S. thesis, McMaster University, 1994).

reading of the membership rosters will illustrate that such associations actually show little direct participation of most members, but a high degree of indirect involvement and identification such as payment of dues and citation of the association on a personal résumé.

Identification with the stated values of an association is an important factor for the membership of religious voluntarism. In a culture of diffuse values characteristic of twentieth-century Western nations, value focus and clarification becomes an important objective. In nations like the United States and Canada, where official government and public policy on religious matters is pluralistic, voluntary religious associations help to clarify. Persons may need to express their theologically distinctive opinions and join or form a voluntary association. In the United States, for instance, evangelical United Methodists in 1966 formed the Forum for Scriptural Christianity (the Good News Fellowship), and American Baptists have a Charismatic Caucus and an Evangelical Fellowship. In Canada, this type of association has taken shape among the mainstream Maritime Baptists with the Atlantic Baptist Fellowship, and within the United Church as the "Community of Concern." Others may wish to practise some ritual regularly or may seek to modify public policy or practise, such as prayer in public schools or the "right to life" movement, and will thus join the Moral Majority or Planned Parenthood. The moral questions of slavery, war, women's rights, and freedom of religion have all benefitted from voluntary associations with religious foundations, as have relatively more limited-in-scope issues, such as animal vivisection, children's reading habits, and protection for young boys working as chimney sweeps.

Of course, the possibility of nominal membership in an association allows for, and may even promote, loose affiliation for purposes of mere identification. Sociologists recognize this level of involvement as "mass donors," in contrast with official formal membership and active participation.[34] Such persons may wish to contribute a minimal sum to achieve a place on the membership roster, while never becoming involved in the actual work of the association or its decision making. In fact, studies have shown that

34. Smith and Reddy, "Overview of Determinants . . . ," 310.

mass donors are quite unlikely and constitutionally unable to participate practically in the association. This type of participation by financial contribution does signal certain social, theological, or even political orientations, as well as legitimating certain personal income tax deductions in appropriate contexts.

IV. Pathologies of Religious Voluntary Associations

Several areas of problematic behaviour or structural difficulty may afflict religious voluntary associations.[35] These include oligarchism, goal displacement, ideological constraint, and competition.

The American sociologist Robert Michels (1876-1936) identified the so-called iron law of oligarchy. By this Michels meant that an aristocratic tendency may manifest itself and, as a result of organization, groups become naturally divided into a minority of directors and a majority of directed.[36] Among religious associations, the oligarchic tendency can be maintained by assumed theological legitimation, manipulation of leadership succession processes, or lack of leadership training opportunities, any of which may lead to organizational pathology. Some leaders can assume a sense of religious "calling" to their leadership positions that overrides due process, or they may adopt a superior theological attitude toward others in the association. Some leadership styles are simply exclusive, holding that only an elite or "elect" are given the gifts of administration and leadership and that all candidates to succeed in office must exhibit the same character or beliefs as the incumbents. This can be a tendency of ordained persons or persons of a particular theological perspective. Still other leaders may remain in positions of leadership so long that the routine rotation that encourages

35. The material here is an application of the categories suggested in Edward A. Ross, "The Diseases of Social Structures," *American Journal of Sociology* 24 (Sept. 1918): 139-58.

36. Robert Michels, *Political Parties: A Sociological Study of the Oligarchical Tendencies of Modern Democracy,* trans. Eden Paul (New York: The Free Press, 1962), 342-56.

voluntary involvement is nullified and no new persons are given any experience in decision making, procedures management, or assessment. Reasons for leaders to retain control beyond reasonable limits include ego satisfaction and a desire to protect the social status that the leaders have earned, along with any possible economic implications.[37] Finally, some leaders may assume in themselves all the significant tasks or more authority than constitutionally granted. This, too, may mitigate against broader voluntary participation. Abrupt restoration of legitimate leadership selection processes (itself an illustration of the voluntary impulse) usually results in overturning the oligarchic tendency.

Goal displacement may also occur within an association. It stands to reason that if the highest level of participation and effectiveness of an association occurs when the objective is most sharply defined, then, as other internal objectives take priority, the association withers and effectiveness is diminished. Internal objectives may include preoccupation with business process and procedures, conflict between leaders, theological diversion, or simply the multiplication of objectives. Radical reclamation of the original purpose is frequently sufficient to restore vitality.

Ideological constraint — in religious terms "theological coercion" — is an identifiable pathology, particularly among Protestants in Britain and North America. Leaders in the evangelical tradition have often been accused of wresting control of organizations from an older elite and protecting their grip through "evangelical dynastic succession." Likewise, theologically liberal traditions may object to intrusions of conservative or evangelical leadership in their associations and behave in the same manner. In both cases, the most likely results are either continual power struggles or the emergence of a new voluntary association made according to the ideologically estranged elite. In these cases, ideological consensus is usually the primary determinant.

Among religious groups, the association may take legitimate disciplinary action against a member who, from the member's point

---

37. Michels, 205-11. Michels also found that the longer the tenure of a leader, the greater the control over the organization.

of view, is organizationally coercive. Where personal influence and dynamics determine the rewards of voluntary association, privileges of the association may be reduced in the face of deteriorated relationships.

Summary

Religious voluntary associations are formed in the same manner as other voluntary associations. The reasons for personal involvement in a voluntary association are often the same as with other categories of associations. Religious associations tend to enjoy a greater sense of urgency than others might, and those involved may perceive a sense of religious calling in their membership. Pathologies of religious associations follow the patterns suggested in other associations, excepting the tendency to be sensitive to theological antagonisms.

CHAPTER SEVEN

Church and "Parachurch": Institution Versus Association

Since the middle of the twentieth century a particular phenomenon of western Christianity has been the so-called parachurch. What this relatively recent term actually applies to is an organizational tradition of Christian associations that lie outside the church in terms of structure and accountability. They may have begun as simple voluntary associations, but many have developed complex organizational models that mingle voluntarism with corporate characteristics. The parachurch organizations rely heavily upon personnel in the churches, imitate certain functions of the church, and may be perceived by church leaders to be competitive.[1] Some writers prefer to define parachurch organizations by their essentially "not-for-profit" tax status, which limits the definition to a certain stage of development and also to the American context.[2]

Parachurch organizations are often equated with voluntarism, when actually these latest examples are an historical subset of the overall voluntary tradition, chronologically later than older, denominational forms (see Chapters Three and Four). Some writers find the roots of the parachurch movement in seventeenth-century An-

---

1. Jerry White, *The Church and the Parachurch: An Uneasy Marriage* (Portland, Ore.: Multnomah Press, 1983), 19, 64.
2. Edward J. Hales and J. Alan Youngren, *Your Money/Their Ministry* (Grand Rapids, Mich.: Eerdmans, 1981).

glican societies, but are uncomfortable about referring to these as any more than "seeds." Others hold to a "William Carey thesis," which places the birth of voluntary associations with the founding of the Baptist Missionary Society in 1792. Still others term the phenomenon an American "Marshall Plan" for meeting the spiritual needs of the post–World War II world.[3] Chronologically, the para-church should properly be dated from the late 1940s.

Ralph Winter (1924-), a well-known missiologist, described the distinction between church and parachurch as one of "modality" and "sodality." He found two distinct types of "redemptive structures" in the New Testament — the "church" and what he refers to as the "missionary bands." The New Testament "church," stated Winter, was basically a Christian synagogue, gathered as normal biological families in aggregate. In contrast, St. Paul's "missionary bands" involved a commitment by those involved, beyond their church relationship, to a specific task. As such, these bands were the prototype of all subsequent missionary endeavours. By the beginning of the medieval period, the church had become a formal diocesan structure, while the monasteries and various sorts of *peregrini* had developed as instances of evangelization and the pursuit of spirituality. Winter suggested that the term "modality" be applied to those diocesan or official, formal structures with no limits on age or sex, while a

3. The "Carey thesis" is a tradition amongst Baptists and evangelicals, traced through Kenneth Scott Latourette to S. Pearce Carey. On this thesis, see my article "The B.M.S. in Proper Context: Some Reflections on the Larger Voluntary Religious Tradition," *The Baptist Quarterly* 34 (1992): 364-78. On the tenuous connection with the Anglican societies, see J. Alan Youngren, "Parachurch Proliferation: The Frontier Spirit Caught in Traffic," *Christianity Today* 6 (November 1981): 38-41; similarly on the eighteenth-century hypothesis, see Richard Lovelace. The idea of a "Marshall Plan," inspired by the U.S. foreign aid policy to rebuild Europe in 1948 and after and named for General George C. Marshall, is found in Ron Wilson, "Parachurch: Becoming Part of the Body," *Christianity Today* 19 (September 1980): 18-20. See also Bruce L. Shelley, "Parachurch Groups (Voluntary Societies)," in *Dictionary of Christianity in America*, ed. Daniel J. Reid (Downers Grove, Ill.: Inter-Varsity Press, 1990), 863-65; Howard Snyder, *The Problem of Wineskins* (Downers Grove, Ill.: InterVarsity Press, 1975); and White, *Church and Parachurch*.

4. Ralph D. Winter, "The Two Structures of God's Redemptive Mission," *Missiology: An International Review* (1974): 127.

"sodality" involved an adult "second decision" beyond modality and involved limitations of age, sex, or marital status.[4] Winter's typologies have received wide attention in the Protestant missiological community, particularly among the independent and evangelical organizations, because he asserted that the sodality principle was recovered in Protestantism and is best exemplified in the modern voluntary associations of the missionary movement.[5]

Close to the pattern suggested by Ralph Winter, sympathetic theologians and several representatives from within the parachurch movement make a case for the parachurch within the church. By first delineating between the local congregation and the universal church, all congregations become a type of "parachurch body."[6] Next, those extracongregational associations that can be adduced from the early church to the modern parachurch ministries become the equivalents of congregations in that they perform the tasks of Christian mission and fill the gaps in local church life. Such manifestations emerge particularly during periods of revival.[7] Typically, this approach is useful as an apologetic within the parachurch community.

Yet another more recent approach to understanding "parachurch" phenomena was advanced by social scientist Robert Wuthnow. Wuthnow cautiously avoided both the parachurch terminology and that of voluntary associations. He preferred instead to speak of "special purpose groups" that have emerged in the United States since World War II. These organizations are shaped by specific objectives, and their tactics involve accumulating resources to achieve their objectives. Similar to other historians of missions, and at counterpoint with many American religious historians, he con-

---

5. A full explication of Winter's hypotheses is found in his presidential address to the American Society of Missiology in 1978: "Protestant Missionary Societies: The American Experience," *Missiology: An International Review* 7:2 (April 1979): 139-78.

6. Emil Brunner, "The Spiritual Center of the Campus Christian Association," *Intercollegian* (April 1955); Karl Barth, "The Church."

7. For instance, see Charles J. Mellis, *Committed Communities* (Pasadena, Calif.: William Carey Library, 1976); Michael Green, *Evangelism in the Early Church* (London: Hodder and Stoughton, 1970); John Briggs, "The Churches and the Parachurch Societies," *Christian Graduate* (September 1978): 4-8.

tended for the sixteenth-century origins of the organizational tradition, with a long history "alongside churches and denominations as ways of advancing Western religion." Wuthnow's analysis is most intriguing because it supports his overall thesis that such religious organizations have played a major role in the restructuring of American religion.[8]

The social interaction between church and parachurch is, therefore, more than it may appear. Historic church institutions have long resented the emergence of parachurch forms because of competition and fear of displacement. Parachurch bodies frequently set themselves against church institutions as being inherently unresponsive and formal, hoping to attract the disinherited or disconcerted. Before proceeding to examine the dynamics between the church and the parachurch, it is useful to review the functions generally associated with each. Basically, the church was established as a theological community for five purposes: (1) fellowship, (2) worship, (3) nurture, (4) discipline, and (5) mission. In contrast, parachurch organizations have emerged essentially around four functions: (1) mission, (2) education, (3) humanitarian concerns, and (4) theologically distinct identification.

I. Definition and Functions of the Contemporary "Church"

By definition, the church is an organized body of human beings that fosters, preserves, renews, and expresses religious sentiments and values — in this case specifically Christian beliefs and values.[9] Christian theologians use metaphors like "Israel of God," "elect of God,"

---

8. Robert Wuthnow, *The Restructuring of American Religion: Society and Faith Since World War II* (Princeton, N.J.: Princeton University Press, 1988), 101.

9. See David O. Moberg, *The Church as a Social Institution: The Sociology of American Religion* (Grand Rapids, Mich.: Baker Book House, 1984), 4ff., for this definition. Of course, there are numerous examples of church and churchly organizations that perform as Christian groups do; however, for the context of this discussion, I am limiting my discussion to Christian examples.

"Body of Christ," and "Royal Priesthood" to describe the theological identity of the church.[10]

Historians, theologians, and other analysts of the church are able to identify the classic and evolved functions associated with the organized church. These are drawn originally from New Testament apostolic teachings, with additional embellishment from the later historical development of the organized church. The first function, the church's fellowship task, expressed in the theological term *koinonia*, pertains to bringing people together to provide social integration. Classic biblical passages that elucidate this function are Matthew 18:19-20; Mark 13:13-31; Romans 12:3-8; 1 Corinthians 12; and Ephesians 2:11-22. In modern Christian groups, fellowship involves worship, the Eucharist, work, mission, and recreation. Within the contemporary structures of a church organization, fellowship can be formalized in committees, small groups, prearranged events, official programmes, and sometimes symbolically in worship services, as with the ritual "right hand of fellowship." In the North American church, testimony meetings, prayer meetings, and cell groups related to a congregation are historic examples of intimate *koinonia*.

Worship, *doxologia*, is also a key function, involving both individual and collective behaviours. Prayer, adoration of God, the celebration of the sacraments/ordinances, and other forms of self-expression in music, drama, and so on, central to Christian spirituality, all contribute to the sense of self-worth of a church member. Stemming from the Pauline instructions in 1 Corinthians 11:23-26, the church has taken to itself the authority to ensure the proper administration of the Lord's Supper. Likewise, the church rightly administers baptism according to the metaphors of Romans 6:1-4. During the Reformation period, the phrase "the true church exists where the word is preached and the sacraments rightly administered"

---

10. See, for instance, Alan Richardson, *An Introduction to the Theology of the New Testament* (New York: Harper and Row, 1958), 266-86; Donald Guthrie, *New Testament Theology* (London: Inter-Varsity Press, 1981), 701-89; George Eldon Ladd, *A Theology of the New Testament* (Grand Rapids, Mich.: Eerdmans, 1974), 342-56, 531-49.

continued to legitimate the sacramental role of the churches. Key biblical passages illustrating worship functions of the community in terms of adoration, prayer, and music are the Torah, the Psalms in the Old Testament, and the organizations of the Gospels and the Book of Revelation in the New Testament.[11]

A third function of the church is nurture, or care of its members. The Greek term *poimen,* expresses this dimension and is accurately rendered "shepherding." Through the pastoral and lay ministries, nurture includes guidance, healing, care for souls, visitation, counselling, and friendship. While some writers consider this function associated primarily with the pastoral office, Anabaptists, contemporary Free Church advocates, and post–Vatican II Catholics consider nurture to be a legitimate function of the church as a body.[12] Key biblical foundations for nurture include Ephesians 4:32 and John 10.

Discipline, *nouthesia,* is a function of the church that provides accountability and identification to the membership. Confession, offerings, correction of aberrant behaviours, and other sanctions provide members with a clear sense of being within the bounds of normative Christianity. In the New Testament context, this involves admonition, reproof, and instruction to bring about voluntary correction.[13] Jesus set the pattern for reproof or discipline in passages like Luke 17. Likewise the Apostles were quite clear in their encouragement of this function: for instance, Paul's correspondence

11. The best survey of the worship function of the church in its various aspects is Ralph P. Martin, *Worship in the Early Church* (Grand Rapids, Mich.: Eerdmans, 1964), esp. 9-18.

12. Compare Thomas Oden, *Pastoral Theology* (San Francisco: Harper and Row, 1972), 190-92, with Melvin J. Steinbron, *Can the Pastor Do It Alone?* (Ventura, Calif.: Regal Books, 1987), 39-45; C. W. Brister, *Pastoral Care in the Church* (San Francisco: Harper and Row, 1992), 102-10; and Siang-Yang Tan, *Lay Counselling: Equipping Christians for a Helping Ministry* (Grand Rapids, Mich.: Zondervan Publishing House, 1991), 23-32, 82-96. On the modifications in Catholic pastoral leadership, see Joseph Gremillion and Jim Castelli, *The Emerging Parish: The Notre Dame Study of Catholic Life Since Vatican II* (San Francisco: Harper and Row, 1981), and Loughlan Sofield and Donald H. Kuhn, *The Collaborative Leader: Listening to the Wisdom of God's People* (Notre Dame, Ind.: Ave Maria Press, 1995).

13. Oden, 206ff.

with the church at Rome (Rom. 15), with the Corinthian church (1 Cor. 5 and 6), and his young friend Timothy (1 Tim. 5 and 6) illustrates the early instructions concerning church discipline.

Mission, *euangelion,* is the term applied in a churchly context to inviting new adherents to the faith community and involving people in the witness and service implied in the gospel. Mission can include evangelism (also defined as increasing the membership of a congregation), care giving, study and support of outreach work, support of and involvement in community and domestic work, and educational ministries, such as a Christian school. Many church bodies have understood the classic mission passages in the New Testament such as Matthew 28:19, 20 to apply to the church as a whole and thus to justify institutional policies concerning mission.[14]

Another way of understanding the theological functions of a church in the biblical context is with reference to spiritual "gifts." The early churches believed that specific gifts or capacities for leadership were given by the Spirit to the churches of the New Testament, and these are usually derived from an analysis of three passages: Romans 12, 1 Corinthians 12, and Ephesians 4. In Romans 12, the apostle lists nine gifts given for the functioning of the churches: prophecy, service, teaching, exhortation, generosity, leadership, mercy, love, and hospitality. Similarly, for the Corinthian church, the list includes nine gifts: wisdom, knowledge, faith, healing, miracles, prophecy, ecstatic utterances, interpretation of utterances, and distinguishing of spirits. And for the church at Ephesus, offices are related to gifts: apostles, prophets, evangelists, pastors, and teachers. Historically, biblical theologians and interpreters for the church have found in these passages a foundation for understanding the appropriate functions of "church."[15]

14. This churchly assumption was the focus of the New School/Old School division amongst American Presbyterians in the 1830s. See Maurice W. Armstrong, Lefferts A. Loetscher, and Charles A. Anderson, eds., *The Presbyterian Enterprise: Sources of American Presbyterian History* (Philadelphia: Westminster Press, 1956), 149-51.

15. Oden, 73-81.

Fellowship, worship, nurture, discipline, and mission, then, summarize the primary functions of a church organization. When the church becomes dysfunctional in any of these areas, Christians may exercise their freedom of choice to find another church relationship or supplement their church membership with an association or organization that meets their particular needs. This can be an association that grows out of the church body or one that is considered "parachurch" by the definition below.

II. Definition and Functions of "Parachurch"

Briefly defined, the parachurch organization is a particular group of voluntary associations of Christians whose purpose is directed at a stated task, relying heavily upon laypersons and independent of any accountability to an institutional church structure, but that may assume functions historically associated with the church. The term "parachurch" literally means "instead of," or, for many, "alongside," the church. Parachurch strategies and structures may be applied to various forms of missions, humanitarian efforts, and educational ventures. Typically, in the North American context, parachurch ministries do not allow for much involvement of the actual membership, preferring instead to collect support from a broad cross section and to leave the administration and policy making to a handful of leaders (who usually derive income from another related enterprise) and paid staffs. Thus, a semblance of voluntary involvement continues, while concessions are made to efficiency and a business model of organizational management.

Parachurch organizations vary widely and do not represent any pure types. It is helpful, therefore, to assess these organizations in light of organizational features.[16] The life cycle for religious voluntary associations, discussed above, must be modified to fit the peculiarities of the parachurch structural development. Most parachurch

16. I am indebted here to the work of James Schultz, "The Voluntary Society and Its Components," in David H. Smith, *Voluntary Action Research: 1972* (Lexington, Mass.: Lexington Books, 1972), 25-38.

organizations begin as simple, relatively informal voluntary associations. As the goals of the association expand and/or the assets and procedures increase and become more complex, the association metamorphoses (cf. the discussion regarding the Bible society model in Chapter Five). The association becomes "established," that is, a service ideal requires procedures and paid staff to achieve the goal of the association. What keeps such an "established voluntary association" (EVA) still voluntary is its continuing ability to tap volunteers and the continuing need to observe democratic proceduralism. Many sociologists observe that most Protestant denominational bodies in the United States and Canada tend to be EVAs, as are organizations like the Southern Christian Leadership Conference and the Women's Christian Temperance Union.[17] In this regard, both the denominational bodies and the independent organizations operate "alongside" the local congregations.

Still other parachurch organizations move to a new stage of complexity, namely that of the "quasi-voluntary organization" (QVO). Here the service ideal is predominant and the organization observes commercial or governmental protocols and is less responsive to its voluntary constituency. The quasi-voluntary religious organization is in short a private nonprofit with a stated goal of a charitable kind involving a specified constituency. Typical of the QVO is the use of volunteers for fund-raising, ceremony, or public relations. Quasi-voluntary parachurch bodies are managed by salaried professionals (not necessarily the elected officers of the organization); they observe the government requirements of nonprofits; and they are assessed according to their service results and growth rate. This category is exemplified in the Y.M.C.A. of old[18] and many of the more recent parachurch organizations, including InterVarsity Christian Fellowship, World Vision, and the United Bible Societies.

Whatever the organizational metamorphic level of the association, parachurch organizations (or ministries, as some observers prefer) provide important functions in Christian endeavour. A brief survey will highlight these functions.

17. Schultz, 34.
18. Schultz, 35.

1. Mission

One of the primary functions assumed by parachurch organizations is to provide for new outlets of mission work. In this regard, the parachurch takes to itself a function historically assumed by the church. This may involve the same variety of missionary work conducted in the church, that is, preaching, church planting, translation of Scripture, and the like. Of primary importance to the parachurch is mission as evangelism. A frequent criticism of the institutional church is that it places greater emphasis upon fellowship and service among the membership than recruitment of new members, or evangelism. As the critique goes, churchly missionary bodies of the last century early turned to institutional management and support over personal "soul winning." Consequently, voluntary associations that coalesce around various forms of evangelism constitute a primary parachurch objective. Examples of evangelism-focused organizations include Campus Crusade for Christ, the Billy Graham Evangelistic Association, Euroevangelism, and the World Evangelical Fellowship.

2. Education

An often overshadowed function of parachurch organizations is education or leadership development. Here again, the parachurch has moved into the functional area of churches described above as "nurture." Education for the parachurch occurs in two ways, within an organization and in a school that caters specifically to a parachurch constituency.

Within each of the parachurch organizations, a certain degree of leadership development takes place. This occurs as role models are imitated in official positions and also as training events are held and specialists are brought in to enhance the qualities of lay leadership. The recruitment of gifted persons with leadership experience also seems to have a salutary effect upon development within the voluntary organization. Within the parachurch organization, these aspects do not differ materially from the general patterns of voluntary associations discussed in Chapter Five.

Leadership development for the parachurch may also be formalized in training institutes, colleges, and seminaries. The paradigm for parachurch educational institutions is old in the heritage of North American Christianity. In the early nineteenth century, countless denominational schools, colleges, and seminaries were started as voluntary associations. In turn, these schools often served the needs of denominational and other churchly voluntary societies. Congregationalists, Baptists, the Christian Church (Disciples of Christ), and some Methodists are examples of this use of voluntary strategy.[19] As the independent missionary boards and associations began to populate American and Canadian Christianity at the turn of the century, new institutions sensitive to the needs and ethos of the parachurch emerged. The clearest example of such institutions were the Bible colleges. The first such schools were Moody Bible Institute in Chicago (1887) and, in Canada, the Toronto Bible Training Institute (1895). Both of these schools and many that came after them specifically met the personnel needs of the parachurch ministries in their respective nations.

In addition to the Bible colleges, the Christian college movement to a certain extent has also been much strengthened in the United States and Canada with parachurch influences. Those with a particular affinity to the parachurch movement are Wheaton College (1881), Houghton College (1883), Nyack College (1882), Gordon College (1889), and Biola University (1908). In Canada, Providence College (1925) and Redeemer College (1975) evince parachurch influences.

Beyond the Bible colleges and undergraduate colleges are theological schools that have exhibited a parachurch sensitivity. In the 1920s, it became obvious to the evangelical community that the older schools did not provide a theologically acceptable programme for their churches and missionary bodies, so many of the same persons who brought into being the first independent mission asso-

---

19. See, for instance, the formation of what became Colgate University in Howard D. Williams, *A History of Colgate University 1819-1969* (New York: Van Nostrand Reinhold Company, 1969), 7-14, and Ernest C. Marriner, *The History of Colby College* (Waterville, Maine: Colby College Press, 1962).

ciations helped to form parachurch theological schools. Among the Baptists were the Eastern Baptist Theological Seminary (1925) and Gordon Divinity School (1931); among Methodists, Asbury Theological Seminary (1923); among Presbyterians, Westminster Theological Seminary (1929) and Covenant Theological Seminary (1957). Other significant institutions that emerged directly from parachurch ministries were Fuller Theological Seminary (1947), Dallas Theological Seminary (1925), the restructured Trinity Evangelical Divinity School (reorg. 1946), and, in Canada, the Briercrest Schools (1935), Regent College (1969), and Ontario Theological Seminary (1978).

3. Theological Distinctiveness

A third function of parachurch organizations is to enable persons to function in a theologically distinctive way. An important example of the need to be distinctly evangelical is in the area of student mission work. This example, by the way, nullifies the thesis that the parachurch is exclusively a post–World War II phenomenon, although the parachurch phase of the organizational evolution began at the mid-twentieth century.

The formal organization of the Young Men's Christian Association in 1858 marks the birth of this important voluntary Christian endeavour. In 1888, under the influence of Dwight L. Moody (1837-1899) and other evangelists, campus groups that had been meeting in places as diverse as Princeton in the United States and Cambridge in England coalesced to become the Student Volunteer Movement for Foreign Missions (S.V.M.). This voluntary impulse was to experience phenomenal growth: within three years over six thousand volunteers met in an international conference, and hundreds were recruited for overseas missionary work with various denominational and ecumenical agencies. Within another seven years, the World's Student Christian Federation had been formed, with John R. Mott (1865-1955) as its first secretary. Collectively the new movement came to be known as the Student Christian Movement (S.C.M.).

Within the first two decades of the new century, however, the S.C.M. suffered a gradual decline. The growth of student populations, theological modernism (particularly the emphasis upon the social gospel over personal evangelism), the First World War, and the advance of denominationally oriented and sponsored campus ministries led to a reorganization of S.C.M. itself and much less support by volunteers. The situation became ripe for critique and redirection.

In 1919, at Cambridge, England, a deep concern for student evangelism emerged in the Cambridge Intercollegiate Christian Union. Young student leaders, notably Noel Palmer (1897-1992), reestablished prayer meetings and Bible studies and helped to broaden their organization to other locations. Their critique of the S.C.M. was direct: the new leaders wanted to return the S.C.M. to a more definitively evangelical doctrinal stance, particularly on matters like the authority of Scripture, the atonement of Christ, and the need for personal Christian experience.[20] The voluntary Keswick movement provided a helpful forum to give shape to what became in 1928 the Inter-Varsity Fellowship of Evangelical Unions, later known simply as InterVarsity Christian Fellowship. The ethos of InterVarsity has remained solidly biblical in theological content, discipling in strategy, voluntary in support, and "disdainful of spiritual superficiality and organized religiosity."

InterVarsity was not the only critique response to mainstream voluntary student work. In 1925, amidst the theological furor in the Presbyterian community in the United States, J. Gresham Machen (1881-1937) and others began a voluntary association of seminary students at Princeton Theological Seminary "to raise up a student protest" against modernist theological trends in the major denominations and schools across America. Later associated with Westminster Theological Seminary in Chestnut Hill, Pennsylvania, the League of Evangelical Students (LES) was dominated by theological students and faculty and often strident in its critique of both liberalism and other evangelical efforts. Another voluntary effort was the Inter-Collegiate Gospel Fellowship, formed in the late 1930s by southern and midwestern interests. The I.G.F. was critical of the InterVarsity movement, preferring to provide for ordained ministers instead of

---

20. Keith and Gladys Hunt, *For Christ and the University: The Story of Intervarsity Christian Fellowship of the U.S.A. 1940-1990* (Downers Grove, Ill.: InterVarsity Press, 1991). Chapters one and two recount the reaction to the S.C.M.

lay workers to do student work. Following a merger with the League, the I.G.F. disappeared after World War II.[21] A result, then, of the critique function of parachurch voluntarism can be a focussed effort in a particular area of ministry, in this case with university students.

4. Humanitarian Concerns

Fourthly, parachurch organizations may develop for Christians to meet a humanitarian concern, like hunger or disaster relief. Due either to overriding administrative priorities or the rapid rise of the stated need, many concerns are neglected by the institutions. Historically these include prisoners, physically disadvantaged persons, the unemployed, the poor, and victims of disasters. In contemporary society, this could include racial groups, gender-defined groups, the institutionalized of one sort or another, and the politically disadvantaged.

Among those evangelicals in the United States parachurch community dedicated to experimental concerns, two organizations stand out: the Sojourners Community and Evangelicals for Social Action. In 1971, Jim Wallis (1948-), a seminary student at Trinity Evangelical Divinity School in Illinois, started a community called the People's Coalition to address social injustices, first in Chicago and later based in Washington, D.C. The community developed a discipleship lifestyle and addressed issues of military conflict, materialism, and racism. An informal association is nurtured by an international magazine called *Sojourners*. Similarly, the Evangelicals for Social Action, founded in 1978 by Ronald J. Sider (1939-), seeks to address various forms of injustice and inequity and to proclaim a holistic biblical lifestyle. These experimental groups have created great interest in the larger Christian community and have modified the social action programmes of several mainline denominations.

A prime example of the parachurch organizational emergence in response to a human need is World Vision and similar predecessors. During the last stages of World War II, for instance, American evangelicals created World Relief (1944) to provide resources for

21. Hunt, 72, and documents at Westminster Theological Seminary Library in Philadelphia.

what was becoming an obviously overwhelming relief demand. A major thrust in this regard occurred when Robert W. Pierce (1914-1976), a California layman, founded World Vision International in 1950 to meet emergency needs in crisis areas of the world through existing evangelical agencies. Its objectives include Christian leadership development, emergency aid, social welfare, and evangelistic outreach in nineteen countries. In 1965, World Vision, in cooperation with Fuller Theological Seminary, created Missions Advanced Research Communications Center (MARC) to provide data on world circumstances. As of the mid-1990s, World Vision distributed over $200 million annually.

Similar to this kind of voluntary humanitarian vision was the founding of Feed the Children, now a major parachurch organization. In 1979, a Baptist minister in Oklahoma City visited Haiti and was moved by the plight of children there. Larry Jones (1940-) used his extensive television ministry to form a coalition of supporters to collect surplus food to send to Haiti. By the mid-1990s, Feed the Children had built a relief network involving corporations and government agencies in its worldwide compassion ministry. A Canadian Society of Feed the Children was opened in Vancouver in 1985 and maintains an active volunteer programme in conjunction with its American counterpart.

In the British Christian tradition, the voluntarist response to aid and refugee problems has been both churchly and parachurch. The churchly model is reflected in Christian Aid, which employs volunteers both in service and in fund-raising, but is connected to the Council of Churches for Britain and Ireland. A parachurch example devoted to self-development and relief is The Evangelical Alliance Relief Fund (TEAR), formed in 1968.

III. Relationships between Church and Parachurch

It would be a mistake to limit the discussion of the parachurch experience to individual organizations and types. Beyond the particular history of these organizations lies a collective sense of the "parachurch as concept." Individual involvement in parachurch organization has been so rewarding for some and so expansive for many of its leaders that it becomes a primary outlet for religious interests and participation. If one observes the kinds of participation a member makes to the life and object of a parachurch organization, it is easy to see how the parachurch can become the definitive form of Christian identity for dedicated members. Time sacrificially given, funds regularly contributed, opportunities for spiritual service, ceremonial recognition of leadership, public perceptions of high levels of "Christian commitment," and careful nurture of voluntary commitment with attendant theological rationale all define a new category called "parachurch Christianity." Parachurch Christians have thus become a new force in religious life, as well as a troubling competitor to older, institutional forms.[22]

The dynamics between church and various voluntary associations, therefore, have shifted considerably. In nineteenth-century voluntary Christianity, churches themselves often spawned and nurtured voluntary associations. Leadership was closely connected with, if not identical to, that of the institutional churches. The more recent voluntary phenomenon of parachurch Christianity has more often than not created antagonistic relationships. Now a serious question emerges over parachurch style as mutually supportive or competitive with traditional churchly Christianity. While parachurch organizations do not provide collectively the functions of a church, through the realization of their mostly singular objectives they can overlap in individual functions with church structures. Both churches and parachurches draw upon common resources — financial and personnel. With limited funds available for avocational or leisure-time activities, competition for "religious" support can be intense. Likewise, the claims of both church and parachurch upon key gifted leaders can be overwhelming and conflictual. Further, because the parachurch is often forged in a context of organizational malaise or critique, both the church and parachurch may develop antagonistic attitudes and perceptions about the purposes of the other. The parachurch, with its singular purpose, may appear to outdistance the more diffuse objectives of church structures and programmes, thus

22. Wuthnow, 91-95, 173-80.

144

appearing to be a triumphant form of Christian endeavour. Parachurch missions may legitimate themselves by claiming to have more personnel in mission, or more dollars raised for mission, or a wider field for mission than either a local church or a denominational body. Similarly, parachurch educational institutions are often enrollment-driven and may emphasize greater numbers of students than there are in the older schools. Finally, in recent years, some parachurch organizations have assumed the function of Christian nurture for their constituencies by providing prayer request lists, devotional guides, and Bible study materials. This form of outreach directly connects with the objective(s) of the parachurch organization, but also duplicates materials historically supplied by church-related boards and agencies.

One of the chief areas of prejudice between church and parachurch is the tension between "antiquity" and spontaneity. Most churchly bodies have long since passed through the nascent stages of informal association and first-generation leadership styles. Their corporate or institutional status gives them a sense of continuity and predictability. Many churches have moreover produced theological histories that help to legitimate their identities. Parachurch organizations, on the other hand, have been born recently and display a variety of incipient-stage organizational characteristics. Single, charismatic leaders, the process of leadership succession, stable funding, accountability issues, interfaces with similar associations, and the need to incorporate themselves as nonprofit corporations all evince themselves in the typical early stages of a parachurch evolution. The sheer history of most parachurch bodies is not longer than thirty to forty years. Churches frequently respond to such organizational outcroppings as "upstarts."

Parachurch leadership may also be derived from the ranks of disaffected or disenfranchised church leaders who seize upon the opportunity to exert their leadership over against former relationships. Another leadership-related difficulty is the actual association of parachurch organizations with forms of the church that are themselves antagonistic to mainstream denominationalism. An example of this is a missionary body that is historically linked with "independent" or theologically "fundamentalist" churches.

Finally, because in the popular mind-set parachurch Christianity is often associated with the evangelical movement, nonevangelicals often reject the work of the parachurch as an organizational outworking of an inadequate form or theological tradition. Denominational Christians frequently make a distinction between their own "historically evangelical" traditions and organized "Evangelicalism," which itself becomes a category of new denominationalism.

Summary

The parachurch is a special category of Christian voluntary associations. Most writers validly point out that the terminology "parachurch" has emerged in special circumstances since World War II. Parachurch organizations have begun typically as voluntary associations, but many have been transformed rapidly by their own success into more complex organizations. At the more complex stages, voluntarism plays a less significant role than in true voluntary associations. Thus the parachurch becomes a special category of discussion, particularly related to the North American context.

In general, parachurch terminology has come to dominate the perception and definition of Christian voluntarism, particularly in the North American evangelical community. The functions of church and parachurch must be sorted out and the positive contributions of each recognized. Often distrust and intense competition characterize the relationship between churches and parachurch bodies, which should be replaced with mutual respect and integration of membership and objectives. It cannot be denied that parachurch organizations rely on the defined Christian constituencies of the churches and also that significant numbers of church members participate in parachurch Christianity. A vital and balanced Christian experience must seek to integrate both streams of endeavour in the doctrine of the church.

CHAPTER EIGHT

Voluntarism within the Christian Congregation

Local congregations have long been a primary context of voluntary dynamics, yet little attention has been paid to the impulses involved and how pastoral leadership might make the most effective use of voluntarism. This chapter first explores the evidences of voluntarism in the congregational setting, then suggests some strategies of response and ministry.

I. Congregational Life Dependant upon Voluntarism

As noted above in the discussion of early Christian communities, new converts joined a body of believers by an act of their own free will. Perhaps in response to preaching or a personal invitation from a pastor or friend, one entered a community of faith. Because second and succeeding generations of Christian converts can come into the faith through the nurture of a family, the church has recognized the need for a personal voluntary response to the nurturing process of conversion, which it has variously called "confirmation" or "full membership vows." How a member becomes active in the church is also a matter of voluntary decision: joining small groups, taking leadership roles, engaging in educational experiences, and being elected to positions of leadership are all voluntary processes. In the present churches of North America and Great Britain, the very issue

147

of participation in a local congregation or fellowship has become selectively voluntary, that is, people become involved in a limited number of religious experiences that compete for their limited time and interest. Enduring voluntary participation is less common than earlier in this century. Over its nineteen-hundred-year history, Christianity in its formal and informal expression has relied upon an essentially voluntary participation and association.

As the medieval Catholic church took shape, the concept of a "vow" became a defining factor for membership in the Christian community. The question of vows to affirm membership in a religious congregation appears at first glance to mitigate against the voluntary impulse. By its nature, a "vow" is a "solemn promise or assertion by which one binds oneself to an act, service, or condition." The term "vow" is derived from the Latin *votum,* meaning "to wish." Religious vows are common to the world's religions, Christianity in its various forms being no exception. Both etymologically and experientially, a vow is ultimately a voluntary act that produces self- or circumstantial coercion. Becoming part of a religious order requires taking a vow; and for over a thousand years, this has been a nonreversible process. Joining a congregation in the Protestant traditions involved a voluntary decision that had to be supported by intentional Christian commitment or one's membership lapsed. This was true of the Lutheran and Reformed communities from the sixteenth centuries. In the Free Church traditions in Britain and North America, membership has been entirely voluntary and vows are understood to be personal commitments that, if broken, result in discontinuation of benefits, that is, fellowship, the sacraments, social identity, and the like — desired objectives for most active Christians. Breaking a vow (through either neglect or intention) is a voluntary act that produces a desired result, namely nonparticipation. While vows may impose self-obligation upon the individual, a vow becomes for the congregation or association a definition of membership, which in a voluntary organization unites an association and creates accountability. Practical theologians in the various Free Church traditions seem not to have difficulties with vows, so long as the vows are subject to be broken and are understood to be of mutual benefit.

The evolution of the meaning of the sacraments, too, reinforces a voluntary dynamic. The sacramental system, essentially defined by Thomas Aquinas (1225-1274), was an Aristotelian system of using physical phenomena to transmit the grace of God. Thus bread and wine became the body and blood of Jesus Christ, which when partaken released the recipients from their sins. Likewise, in baptism, the water was seen to wash away or cleanse the original sin of the subject. Because the Church held that there was no salvation outside the Church and that God required faithfulness through the sacraments, a high degree of theological coercion can implicitly be involved. However, if one sees the sacraments as symbols in ceremony of the transitions in life and the attendant benefits thereto accruing, such as a name for a child in baptism or participation in a defined community in Holy Communion, then an element of voluntary response for a desired result is at work. Although baptism administered to infants was not a voluntary act for the one baptized, a case could be made for the voluntary presentation of the child by parents in order for the child to enjoy the spiritual benefits of the sacrament. The other sacraments in the Roman tradition could be seen as partially voluntary in that each depended upon willing human cooperation (penance, marriage, ordination), with the exception of the Last Rites, which were often administered after the recipients were no longer able to make the choice for themselves.

In the Reformation traditions, the churches' ability to place sanctions against those who declined the sacraments was lost, and the two remaining sacraments were offered freely to those who became members of the church by voluntarily taking vows. Baptism, of course, continued to be a voluntary decision of the parents or sponsors, later to be validated by confirmation, while the Lord's Supper was enjoined on the faithful to increase their faith, to use John Calvin's phraseology.[1] Luther commented, "As to the need for faith in the sacraments, I will die before I recant,"[2] emphasizing the voluntary response of a believer, which is in itself a gift of God.

1. John Dillenberger, ed., *John Calvin: Selections From His Writings* (New York: American Academy of Religion, 1975), 213.
2. Quoted in Roland Bainton, *Here I Stand: A Life of Martin Luther* (Nashville, Tenn.: Abingdon Press, 1950), 139.

In much of the modern church, the sacraments (or ordinances, as they are known in some traditions) are by invitation. Parents or sponsors are invited to present their children for infant baptism, which is followed by a voluntary affirmation at an age of account-ability by the person baptized. Among those in the believer's church traditions, baptism is an entirely voluntary act of obedience to Christ and a profession of one's personal faith. Similarly, the ordinance/sacrament of Holy Communion is offered as a means of sacred fellowship and spiritual reflection to those who respond to Christ's invitation to come to the Table. Some writers have also found in the sacraments/ordinances an important model for understanding Christian responsibility. Baptism creates the way in which the church exists and the Lord's Supper creates a household table for the Lord's stewards.[3] Participation in baptism and communion are thus rooted in choices made voluntarily. The life of the community of faith, as witnessed in the sacraments/ordinances, is changed in more ways than are generally assumed.

Stewardship has been variously defined as the responsibility of Christians before God for managing God's creation and resources, a lifestyle of representing God, who owns all things.[4] Applied within the context of local congregational ministry, stewardship means in part the efficient use of resources given through God's people for Christian endeavour. To properly interpret stewardship and to en-hance their responsibility as stewards have been major challenges for ministry,[5] particularly in view of the voluntarism latent in the congregation. The terminology of "tithing" found in the Old Testa-ment law codes (Lev. 27) and prophets (Mal. 3:10) possesses a mildly

3. Ronald E. Vallet and Charles E. Zech, *The Mainline Church's Funding Crisis: Issues and Possibilities* (Grand Rapids, Mich.: Eerdmans and Manlius, N.Y.: REV/Rose Publishing, 1995), 156.

4. Compare, for instance, Douglas J. Hall, *The Steward: A Biblical Symbol Come of Age* (New York: Friendship Press, 1982), 5ff., with John H. Westerhoff, *Building God's People in a Materialistic Society* (New York: Seabury Press, 1983), 20-23.

5. This is the interest of Ronald E. Vallet, *Stepping Stones of the Steward: A Faith Journey Through Jesus' Parables*, 2d ed. (Grand Rapids, Mich.: Eerdmans and Manlius, N.Y.: REV/Rose Publishing, 1994).

coercive tone, while the New Testament suggests a more generous and voluntaristic standard called "cheerful giving" (2 Cor. 9:7). Modern Christian stewardship is altogether based on persuasion in the context of a market-driven benevolence economy. If a person's relationship to the faith community is one of respect, trust, and affection, then it follows that the individual will respond favourably to stimuli to support the church and its objectives, such as a sermon, a financial pledge, or a free-will offering. Fundamental to the building of trust will be the perception that democratic decision making exists and that there is a high level of participation by the membership in determining the use of the collections. Further, if one is convinced of a "call" to support an object, then inner conviction becomes a kind of compulsive voluntary action. Ministers and lay leaders do well indeed to recognize their powers of persuasion to convince a congregational member to respond freely to an opportunity to share personal resources. In this way, leaders appeal to the same personal interests (in this case defined as religious objectives) as any commercial marketing strategy or nonreligious voluntary fund-raising appeal, such as the United Way or Boy Scouts/Girl Guides.

Change comes about in the typical Christian congregation in a variety of ways.[6] External factors such as technology and demographic shifts, denominational pressure, and the normal internal course of events, such as aging of the membership, all bring about deliberate change.[7] Critique or criticism can also bring about change and often reflects a deeper voluntarist force than the issues that are articulated. Accompanying the "real issues" may be feelings of inadequacy, powerlessness, conflict, confusion, and loss.[8] Discontent over the direction of a programme or disaffection with pastoral or

6. The literature on change in the church is rapidly growing. One of the most popular books is Leith Anderson, *Dying for Change: An Arresting Look at the New Realities Confronting Churches and Parachurch Ministries* (Minneapolis, Minn.: Bethany House Publishers, 1991), esp. 109-23.

7. An excellent contemporary resource on organizational change is Lee G. Bolman and Terrance E. Deal, *Reframing Organizations: Artistry, Choice and Leadership* (San Francisco: Jossey Bass, 1991), 368-84. The authors list factors such as globalization, information technology, and deregulation as significant factors.

8. Bolman and Deal, 397.

other leadership will produce discussion and other strategies suggesting undefined change. Malaise or drop in membership or participation can also produce the desire for new direction. During annual meetings, elections, or leadership changes through other means, the first impulse for change may be seen, as in informal clusters or groups that may emerge to voice the need for change. If the structure and/or leadership is unwilling or unable to respond to these initiatives, recognizable voluntary action often results. A committee is formed, reference is made to structures and accountabilities beyond the congregation, or loyalties shift to various types of parachurch associations. The congregation's ability to deal creatively with this type of voluntarism determines whether the impulse is constructive or destructive to its overall life and experience.

Critique may also occur in ways that are unwelcome interferences in the life and ethos of a congregation. For example, new members with theological, ethical, or social perspectives radically different from those of the traditional membership may attempt to transform the church in their image. The impact of Christian fundamentalism often follows this pattern at the local church level, as zealous members advocate a theological position like scriptural inerrancy, attempt to create enforceable doctrinal standards for membership or leadership, or severely criticize the existing leadership until the person(s) is no longer able practically to lead. This type of negative voluntarism presents a formidable challenge to pastors and congregational leadership of the present era.

II. How Ministry Is Geared to Voluntary Participation

Ministry in the congregation is facilitated by several devices, including preaching, worship, mission, pastoral care, and stewardship. Led by both ordained and lay leadership, the ministry of the members of a congregation becomes a fertile field for the expression of Christian voluntarism.

Preaching in the Christian congregation is one of the most potent devices that activates a voluntary response. As shown by the sermons of St. Peter at Pentecost and St. Paul at Mars Hill, the point of the sermon is to initiate change in the hearer, like conversion or a deeper commitment or a new direction in one's Christian experience. A sense of urgency must accompany mere exhortation, noted one classic writer.[9] Listeners to a sermon, Fred Craddock has recently noted, "want room to say no to a sermon, but a genuine invitation to say yes."[10] Preachers consciously attempt to change the behaviour of others who have an ability to act and change. All preaching is by its nature persuasive and reinforces the voluntary dynamic in congregational life.[11]

In much of North American Protestantism and British Nonconformity, the sermon became central to the worship experience and the determination of Christian ethics. Puritans and Pietists relied heavily upon the sermon to educate and motivate a receptive congregation. Later, the revivalists of the eighteenth and nineteenth centuries fully understood their role as divine instruments to call people to radical transformation. Similarly, in Britain and North America, the sermon has been used in activistic traditions to persuade people of a moral or ethical position, such as the evil of slavery or the need to adopt a position on human abortion. Whole institutions grew up around the need to train great preachers, notably Spurgeon's College in Britain and Evangelical Theological School (later Dallas Theological Seminary) in the United States. A substantial number of pastors, then, have been trained through education or experience to view the sermon as an ultimate facilitation of the voluntary response. Noteworthy also is the desire of many laypeople to place themselves in receipt of effective preaching, implicitly asserting their desire to be affected religiously. Few congregations would knowingly select a pastor who is an inadequate preacher; good preaching is a primary determinant in the pastoral call system. For these reasons, the church and the ministry will not soon give up

9. John A. Broadus, *On the Preparation and Delivery of Sermons* (New York: Harper Brothers, 1944), 215.

10. Fred B. Craddock, *Preaching* (Burlington, Ont.: Welch Publishing Co., 1991), 89.

11. J. Daniel Baumann, *An Introduction to Contemporary Preaching* (Grand Rapids, Mich.: Baker Books, 1972), 223-24.

their appreciation of effective preaching, despite the critics of preaching who argue that it is a poor form of monological communication.[12]

Like preaching, worship in most Protestant and many Catholic congregations is responsive to the voluntary impulse. From the eighteenth-century patterns of worship that characterized the majority of mainstream denominations, the typical congregation was "led" in worship according to a style that was clergy-dominant and predictable in liturgy. In the last two decades, however, that style has changed for many congregations to lay-defined, lay-friendly, expressive forms of worship that solicit overt voluntarist behaviour: prayers have become spontaneous, ritual less formal, and music utilized that elicits physical responses like clapping and raising of hands. Provision is made for increased voluntary response throughout the service. Significant sectors of British and North American churches have been transformed by this surge of voluntarism in the laity in defining worship needs and patterns. Only chronologically older church members loyal to more liturgical patterns seem able to resist the trend for the time being. Indeed, what is really at stake in the charismatic tradition and much of the church renewal trends in Christian worship is a newly found Christian voluntarism. Not being responsive to these initiatives frequently creates stress and sometimes unwelcome division in the congregation.

Mission involvement of church members represents a major arena of voluntary participation. Historically, mission has included prayer support, educational nurture, and interpretation of missionary work external to the congregation, plus actual involvement in mission enterprise such as soup kitchens, language classes, visitation of the sick and institutionalized persons, distribution of literature, and personal evangelism. For most of the modern era of Catholic and Protestant congregational missions, mission has been sponsored, interpreted, and conducted through denominational bodies, whether boards or voluntary associations (see Chapter Four).

More recently, voluntary bodies external to the congregation,

---

12. So argued Marion L. Soards in " 'Pulling the Wagon Out of the Ditch': A Biblical Scholar Reads Homiletic," *United Theological Seminary Journal of Theology* 93 (1989): 20-21.

especially parachurch organizations, have targeted the local parish as both a clientele of participants and a source of mission support funds. Often, congregational ideas of mission are quite distinct from those of a parachurch mission agency. Parachurch mission can be focussed upon targeted needs and outreach, while denominational mission is usually more inclusive of a variety of objects. Local congregational members are often poorly informed to make critical assessments for themselves of appropriate channels of mission interests, and they rely heavily upon pastoral or denominational advice. The typical strategy of local church leadership has been to frown upon excessive extra-parish organizational investment at the cost of denominational work. As noted above, with the parachurch, competition between mission claims has resulted in increased voluntarism.

Holistic Christian stewardship includes responding to opportunities to affirm religious ideals through personal resource allocation. Obviously a valuable dimension of voluntarist expression, this is a crucial device for the health and well-being of a parish. In the nineteenth century, stewardship was often expressed in two ways: through offerings collected in the church for use through and primarily for the local parish and special offerings for projects, societies, and special needs. "Designated" giving allowed donors maximum discretion about the use of their gifts. As denominational organizations grew in size and complexity, however, designated giving disadvantaged denominational managers because it lacked predictability, it required excessive accountability, and it allowed unwanted competition for funds in time of scarcity or intensive propaganda.[13] Consequently, the designated giving pattern was gradually replaced in the mid-twentieth century by a more comprehensive unified budget plan adopted by most denominational programmes to facilitate single distribution of funds and receipting processes demanded by charitable gift deductions in the personal income tax codes. Membership convenience was also a factor in that transition. While the unified system worked well for coordination and administration of funds as well as financial planning in the local church, it presented

13. Vallet and Zech, 79ff., describes the various scenarios of giving patterns.

a diffuse case for ministers to persuade donors to maintain or increase their contributions. Most denominations in recent decades have been forced to modify the unified stewardship system in response to voluntary impulses to allow for the older, more designated strategy of giving.

Church administration becomes a significant area of leadership when pastor and lay leaders are confronted with spontaneous voluntary behaviour. By "church administration" in this context is meant the leadership that pastors and laypersons give in facilitating the mission and objectives of a congregation and their response to voluntarist initiatives. It is evident from a study of the New Testament churches and the subsequent development of the medieval Catholic Church and Protestantism that good leadership has enabled the church to survive and be faithful to its Lord and mission.[14] Appropriate, noncoercive church administration in the contemporary congregation involves seeking consensus from within the body, "reading" voluntary impulses, and evaluating directions and results on a continuing basis.

Pastors as administrators are most effective as servant leaders, serving the congregation and offering vision where new direction and energy are required. Style of leadership is important and should include the ability to reflect, flexibility in changing circumstances, and a clear sense of leadership objectives and values.[15] The expression of leadership initiative needs to be experienced through the congregation, not just as a filter to refine the ideas or strategies, but as part of a process of ownership and accountability. Once decisions are reached, it is equally important to have in place the mechanisms of evaluation that are common to contemporary commercial or government operations. These include regular personnel evaluation, programme assessment, revisioning, regular cycling of

14. An excellent resource that focusses on the evolving issues of leadership in the Catholic tradition is Edward Schillebeeckx, *Ministry: Leadership in the Community of Jesus Christ* (New York: Crossroad Publishing Co., 1981).

15. Jerald W. Apps, *Leadership for the Emerging Age: Transforming Practice in Adult and Continuing Education* (San Francisco: Jossey Bass, 1994), 55-61. For a Roman Catholic perspective, see Thomas Sweetser, *Successful Parishes: How They Meet the Challenge of Change* (Minneapolis, Minn.: Winston Press, 1983).

voluntary leadership, collection of opinion through pastoral care, and interaction of members in open forums and with appropriate persons and constituencies in the larger religious and community cultures. With these ideals and mechanisms in place, when voluntarist impulses arise, there should be genuine openness to alternative possibilities and cooperative, nonthreatening responses from leadership and institutionally protective elements of the congregation. A congregation's sense of internal well-being will present a reasoned and sensitive response to what may be considered interference from external sources of religious change, such as the impact of charismatic or fundamentalist voluntarism as described above. Needless to say, responding to voluntary impulses by rigidity or excessive defensiveness is not indicative of either congregational health or openness to the Spirit's necessary designs to maintain the vitality of the churches.

III. Voluntarism, Postmodernism, and the Congregation

Beginning with the 1970s, a school of aesthetic, philosophical, and literary critique known as "postmodernism" emerged in France and North America. Writers like Jean Baudrillard (1929-), Jacques Derrida (1930-), and others offered a methodological assault on the principles of "modernity," particularly the unities of meaning, theory, and self.[16] Of importance to postmodernists is the downfall of Enlightenment principles of reason, order, structure, and predictability. For postmodern sociologists, unified culture is being splintered into discrete spheres, where there is a desperate need for reunification that, at the same time, is perceived to be an impossibility.

16. On the postmodernist theorists, see Jacques Derrida, *Writing and Difference,* trans. Alan Bass (London: Routledge and Kegan Paul, 1978), 3-30; J. Claude Evans, *Strategies of Deconstruction: Derrida and the Myth of the Voice* (Minneapolis, Minn.: University of Minnesota Press, 1991), xix-xx; Jacques Baudrillard, *In the Shadow of the Silent Majorities, or The End of the Social: and Other Essays* (New York: Semiotext, 1983).

The impact of postmodernism on organizational theory is profound. First, advocates of postmodernism argue that organizational theory itself is a creature of modernity. Max Weber (1864-1920) and others in his tradition held to an inexorable advance of bureaucratic rationality and coordinated institutions, which make up modern societies and economies. Weber was the principal theorist of modernization, and one of his outstanding illustrations was the Western Christian Church. However, the failure of the modern synthesis, the restructuring of commercial and government institutions, and the growth of cybernetics and information systems have all conspired against the survival of bureaucracy. Thus, argue the social theorists, institutions are in need of new, adaptable organizational models. Aside from its theological implications, then, postmodernist critique calls into focus strategies and structures that imply a voluntarist impulse.[17]

What does a postmodernist organization look like? Essentially the inverse of the modern ideal: small subunits whose object is providing service or information, with a flexible labour force and a decentralized, eclectic, participative managerial structure.[18] In short, Christian congregations fit the postmodern ideal neatly. Changing organizations must look to decentralize bureaucracy and empower autonomous or independent units. Another important result of postmodernist critique is a trend away from hierarchical management. Communication is improved and status differences are minimized. For congregations, this may mean a greater application of Free Church polity, especially democratic decision making. A strong case can be made in the postmodern school of thought for the revival of voluntary associations in fresh and unusual forms related to the local congregation as a wave of the future.

The application of postmodern organizational theories to congregational ministry presents several fascinating possibilities. If the conglomerate and macrocosmic organizations and institutions of the

---

17. Paul Thompson, "Postmodernism: Fatal Distraction," in *Postmodernism and Organizations,* ed. John Hassard and Martin Parker (London: Sage Publications, 1993), 184-85.

18. S. Clegg, *Modern Organizations: Organizations Studies in the Postmodern World* (London: Sage Books, 1990), 177.

modern Christian movement are the denominations, then one should look for the downsizing and potential elimination of some denominational relationships. For this reason, some literature in the North American Protestant community has referred to this phenomenon as "post-denominationalism." What is usually meant by this terminology is a critique of denominations by smaller sects and the parachurch organizations, who may be moving to supplant the older or mainline denominations with a new wave of bureaucratic and quasi-coercive organizations. This follows the historic pattern suggested in Chapter Five.

Whether the decline of mainline denominations is ultimately attributable to postmodern deconstruction or to other factors, the relationship of denominations to congregations has implications for voluntarist dynamics. Denominations have emerged in post-Reformation Protestantism from confessional families to "para-local-church" bodies in their own right. Some denominations prefer to understand themselves as "church" like the Lutheran bodies or United Methodists in the United States, while others like the Baptists see extra-congregational organizations as entirely task-oriented and accountable to the congregations. In some cases, there are strict accountability and various forms of coercion (as in the Episcopal Church); in others, the relationship is entirely voluntary (as in the Christian Church [Disciples of Christ]), thus forming another sphere of voluntarist expression. As the demands of mission, education, and other common tasks have become complex and costly, denominations have taken on a life of their own, and voluntary relationships have been supplanted by coercive means. For instance, democratically elected officers and voluntary secretaries have been replaced with executive staff and professional assistants. Voluntary contributions from parishes to regional and national organizations have been replaced by assessments or apportionments. A truer image of post-denominationalism, however, presents the real possibility that many extra-congregational religious organizations will be reduced and some eliminated by their very archaic typology. Thus a "reordering" of Christian endeavour and structures is likely, as sociologist Robert Wuthnow believes. For North American Christians, this will most likely take the shape of a theological subgroup, a common task, and/or a geographically defined affinity group.[19] Database networks will be as significant in making linkages as ceremony and personal fellowship. Participants in the networks of congregations and voluntary associations of the future will be less professional and inclusive of many more categories of laypersons. While some critics of postmodern theory see the movement as a distraction, "a retreat from engagement by sections of the intelligentsia,"[20] there are signs in the Christian community that postmodern organizational "deconstruction" is already being realized.[21]

As religious culture is being restructured, not only in the United States but in Canada and the United Kingdom as well, local congregations must respond creatively. Restructuring will mean at least two changes: substructuring of the congregation itself and addition to the mix of ministry and participatory possibilities. Each of these is relevant to the future vitality of the local congregation.

Small group associations within the congregational community will be the primary participation of most church members of the next generation. Cell groups for spiritual formation and nurture are a common type. These meet regularly and may change in composition on a fairly frequent basis; both interest and needs change, and participants may drop in or out as time and need arise. Few people in contemporary society will have the desire or the time to commit regularly to a specified day for long periods of time. Traditional gender- or age-specific groups have become unacceptable or less desirable. Thus, these new categories of small groups have largely supplanted the former midweek Bible studies, ladies' circles, and

19. Robert Wuthnow, *The Restructuring of American Religion: Society and Faith Since World War II* (Princeton, N.J.: Princeton University Press, 1988), 107-31.

20. Thompson, 202.

21. In the United States, major denominational organizations are being "downsized": American Baptists, United Church of Christ, Presbyterian Church in the U.S.A., and the Christian Church (Disciples of Christ). In Canada, the process is even more dramatic among the "convention" Baptists, Anglicans, Presbyterians, and the United Church of Canada. In the United Kingdom, the list includes the Church of England, the Baptist Union, and the British Council of Churches.

men's fellowship groups. While there are several advantages to these small group associations, including therapeutic interaction, there can be a possibility of highly self-centered religious experience.[22]

A second type of small groups has to do with affinity groups for tasks or common interests for which the church family may still be a defining group. Included here are hobby and recreation groups, health care support groups, physical fitness programmes, senior citizens' groups, and substance-abuse care programmes, to name just a few. Again, the membership will be defined by interest or need, rather than by "rules and dues." The primary role of a local church for all of these small groups is to provide a place of meeting and communication about and among the groups.

In response to the present tendencies toward deconstruction and the emergence of small interest groups, it is incumbent upon those in local church ministries to find a means of effectively using small groups. Leaders would do well to discover the means for attracting new constituencies of voluntary associations into the parish family. Unless there is a theological or ethical reason for not cooperating, the parish structure must remain open to new relationships. Leaders of the associations should be encouraged to enjoy the unique functions of the churches, that is, nurture, education, and the sacraments/worship, and, within reason, should recognize some appropriate level of accountability. Disputes in the voluntary association sector, for instance, could be mediated in a parish context. A redefinition of "church" along these lines not only recalls the circumstances of the primitive Christian era, but also sets a pattern for inclusivity rather than elitism. If analysts are correct in observing the growing tendency toward cybernetic connections through databases and the like, any personal encounter with other Christians will be increasingly desirable. Thus small-group associations will enhance human relationships in the congregation. Moreover, those in professional ministry need to become actively involved in the voluntary sector to allow themselves the easy benefit

---

22. Robert Wuthnow, *"I Come Away Stronger": How Small Groups Are Shaping American Religion* (Grand Rapids, Mich.: Eerdmans, 1994), 344-60, lists as advantages simplicity, diversity, low expense, individual responsibility, and personal spirituality.

of cross-confessional relationships and to direct their support to focussed objects and needs in which their corresponding parish members are likely already involved.

Ultimately, the authority structures of a local parish will change
when interactive with voluntary associations. First, traditionally hierarchical systems of parish leadership (the episcopal, for instance)
will blend to a more congregational style.[23] Second, professional
authority will be diffused to greater lay authority, and lay empowerment will result. Rather than a threat over the loss of prerogatives,
diffusion of leadership may actually become an objective in ministry.[24]

As the structures of authority are transformed in the local
parish, so also will patterns of mission participation and stewardship. Denominations are being greatly reduced in both services
offered and influence enjoyed in this regard. The telling barometer
on the state of health of denomination/congregation relations is the
stewardship results. A recent study has shown that the dramatic
decline in mission receipts may be due to disagreement over mission
priorities and general distrust of denominational leadership.[25]
Rather than defined essentially by a single denominational emphasis, mission will broaden to include a variety of objects and emphases that are likely to attract greater participation from a broader
spectrum. Concomitant with the broadened sense of mission will
be an enlarged collection and distribution of personal resources.
Both of these voluntarist-generated results could in turn lead to a
redefinition of "denomination" to what might be called *nouveaux
ecclesiae,* or new categories of visible Christian witness, intermingling structurally the traditions of the church with the impulse of

23. Among United Methodists in the United States, for instance, local
congregations now have a major role in determining their apportionment payments
to annual conference programmes.

24. American Baptists, for example, over the past two decades have empowered regional leaders, and the denomination has given wide opportunity to
differentiated theological and mission perspectives through their Study Commission on Denominational Structures (SCODS) and the Study Commission on Relationships (SCOR).

25. Vallet and Zech, 85.

the voluntary associations. Such an eventuality, now taking shape in North America and Great Britain amongst many Protestant coalitions, effectively challenges the organized ecumenical models of the first half of the twentieth century.[26]

Summary

The local parish is both the origin and the frontier of the voluntarist impulse. Because Christians are gathered in both congregations and voluntary associations for specific and discrete reasons, the two manifestations of the Reign of God on earth must recognize each other's validity and find ways to cooperate. Voluntarism is transforming the local parish through preaching, worship, mission, and stewardship and externally through the formation and interaction of various voluntary associations. Ministry is impeded by competition and thwarted by unwarranted cynicism about motives of service. Thus the future of effective local church ministries depends upon rapprochement between church and voluntary association. This, it has been argued, creates the possibility of a new spiritual community, the *nouveaux ecclesiae*.

26. Compare the organizational heritage of the ecumenical movement in Willem A. Visser 't Hooft, "The Genesis of the World Council of Churches," in *A History of the Ecumenical Movement 1517-1948*, ed. Ruth Rouse and Stephen Charles Neill (Geneva: World Council of Churches, 1986), 697-725.

CHAPTER NINE

The Enduring Values of Christian Voluntarism

The voluntary tradition has left an indelible imprint on Christianity in Britain and North America. Rooted in a biblical tradition of persuasion and growing from a transformation in understanding of human capability, voluntarism first modified church structures and later created its own organizational forms. Perhaps no other locus better than the local congregation illustrates the continuing impact of the voluntary impulse. Many contemporary writers assert that this tendency may become a dominant feature of collective Christianity in the next decades. Let us then summarize the enduring values of Christian voluntarism.

I. Values Received from Christian Voluntarism

A. Voluntarism Has Brought Empowerment

Churches of a primarily voluntary type and, later, voluntary associations for a variety of religious purposes provided an identity for groups of people otherwise included silently in categories with others. Further, initial opportunities for service, employment, and recognition often came through voluntary channels. Identity, vocation, and recognition are characteristics of empowerment, and no group was assisted more by the voluntary tradition than women.

At the outset of the seventeenth century, the lot of women in England was that of spouse, generally confined to the household. Exceptions to this were widows, servants, social outcasts, and women in religious life. Particularly among certain of the Nonconformist sects, women gained the opportunity to express themselves and act as leaders.[1] Likewise, in the North American colonies, Nonconformist women achieved leadership roles. At the outset of the nineteenth century in the United States, women began to organize missionary societies that gathered significant numbers of women of all ages who found in Christian voluntary associations a release from the domestic scene and an opportunity to become organizers and managers themselves.[2] It has been argued that a primary factor in the emancipation of women was the evolution of the voluntary association.[3]

Empowerment through voluntary organizations for religious purposes extended to many other underrepresented groups. Former slaves in the southern United States organized missionary societies locally and then nationally. Many black preachers found in the voluntary denominations of the eighteenth and nineteenth centuries the chance to "prove" their social worth and gain community status.[4] New immigrants in Canada and the United States formed associations of mutual cultural and religious support to deal with the disorientation of removal from their homelands. Similarly, among immigrant groups such as the Germans, Swedes, Danish-Norwegians, and later Chinese and Japanese, greater opportunity for service occurred within the voluntary mission socie-

---

1. Antonia Fraser, *The Weaker Vessel: Woman's Lot in Seventeenth Century England* (London: Methuen, 1984), 158-79.

2. Ruth A. Tucker and Walter Liefeld, *Daughters of the Church: Women and Ministry from New Testament Times to the Present* (Grand Rapids, Mich.: Zondervan Publishing Co., 1988), 245-327.

3. Joan Jacobs Brumberg, *Mission for Life: The Story of the Family of Adoniram Judson, The Dramatic Events of the First American Foreign Mission, and the Course of Evangelical Religion in the Nineteenth Century* (New York: The Free Press, 1980), 79-106, argued that "Gospel Christianity constituted the feminist revolution."

4. James Melvin Washington, *Frustrated Fellowship: The Black Baptist Quest for Social Power* (Macon, Ga.: Mercer University Press, 1986), 83-103.

ties and the voluntary church forms created specifically for these social groups.[5]

Finally, persons with physical disabilities, those with social and economic disadvantages, widows, orphans, and a host of others were identified in the larger community through the targeted compassion of Christian voluntarism from the early 1800s onward. Admittedly, this is an area where religious voluntarism has resulted in less empowerment than that associated with the political institutions.

B. Voluntarism Has Provided for Experiment

Time and again, the structured permanent forms of Christianity have been slow or reluctant to move into new areas of ministry. Examples of this reluctance are placing the Scriptures in the hands of the common people, taking a controversial moral stance, and extending the geographical boundaries of activity. In the earlier discussion, we have seen how new directions in Christian mission and social concern were achieved first in voluntary associations. Prominent examples of this experimental dimension are the Bible society movement, the antislavery crusade, and, more recently, the growing recognition of gay rights and activism.

The experimental value of voluntary organizations allows temporary associations to respond to spontaneous needs. By its nature, the institutional church is designed to deliberate and plan and develop long-term strategies. Voluntary associations, in contrast, may emerge quickly and develop short-term goals, leadership, and financial resources. Associations bring organizational flexibility not only to the churches but to the social context in general. Some experimental objectives survive and run the course of organizational evolution, as demonstrated above. Others come to the end of the viability of their objectives and die or change purposes. Prime examples of this pattern were the development of antislavery societies within nineteenth-century denominations and the women's suffrage crusade

5. Charles L. White, *A Century of Faith* (Philadelphia: Judson Press, 1932), 244-48.

that ended in suffrage. In each case, the experimental nature of Christian voluntarism was essential to the social or religious context.

C. Voluntarism Has Created New Leadership

The voluntary movement has broadened considerably the involvement of people in Christian endeavour. Where offices and roles within a local congregation may be limited by the oligarchical characteristic, lay voluntarism has risen to meet the demands of countless parachurch organizations and ministries. One of the leading characteristics of the laypersons involved in voluntary associations is catholicity of spirit. Crossing traditional churchly confessions, many associations that focus on an object of interest to a broad spectrum of Christians draw persons of varying theological, social, and political perspectives. Such volunteers derive great personal satisfaction from their engagement with persons of faith communities different from their own. Moreover, they may develop larger senses of the mission of the church than from within a denominational frame of reference. Since associations are composed of individual relationships, in contrast with the collective relationships of congregations, motivation for recruitment of new members is stronger, according to the "Andrew Principle," that is, one person taking the initiative to invite another to join or participate. In response, the attraction of becoming a member through the personal invitation of another is strong.

The media and virtually every imaginable leisure-time organization employ solicitation of a mass kind to increase membership and participation in voluntary associations. With limited resources to apply from disposable income, individuals and families respond to what appeals to them or to which organizations appeal first or most effectively. The application of this principle in religious fund-raising and membership enlistment (evangelism) has long been recognized and even nurtured. The vivid requests of television evangelists and the calculated postal mailings, plus the institutes to train Christian fund-raisers and church growth workers, all point in the same direction: increased voluntary leadership and participation is a permanent and necessary component of the religious community.

D. Voluntarism Has Focussed Mission

One of the great values of the voluntary paradigms wrought in British and North American experience is singularity in purpose. The individualism of English-speaking culture connects best with opportunities designed to satisfy personal initiative. Focus of objective upon a single topic or goal invariably outweighs diffuse objectives. The most enduring result of the voluntarist surge of the nineteenth century was the permanent preoccupation in Protestantism and Catholic churches with various types of mission. Witness that in the immediate context, church extension, education, and overseas obligations became a high priority. By 1830, virtually every denominational body in the United States and Britain had created an association or an internal structure to conduct mission. Later, autonomous mission societies and boards emerged in the Canadian churches, and still later a new wave of independent mission bodies grew up to meet the demands of a new Protestantism. Other legitimate functions of the church, including nurture, worship, and discipline, became lesser priorities.

With the new priority of mission in focus, results became a major determinant of successful voluntarism. Statistical reports, assessments, inducements, and comparative uses of data became standard tools for nurturing the vitality of voluntarist efforts. From the earliest period of church-related voluntary associations like the New England Company and the S.P.C.K., healthy competition and challenges to exceed the achievements of the previous year have characterized voluntary behaviour. This "data processing" and propaganda (some departments were referred to as such!) have become permanent features of denominational as well as local congregational reports, the literary outlets of the voluntary sector, like periodicals, and research centers like MARC. The information disseminated by these operations feeds the large appetite for assessments, strategic planning, and theological reflection. One of the clearest signals that an association or congregation is languishing is the point at which results are not regularly circulated, publications are delayed in production, or statistical trends are noticeably in decline. Many of the mainline denominational organizations have bureaus created just to manage and interpret statistics.

II. What Voluntarism Suggests for the Future

Churches — both local congregations and associative bodies — must respond realistically to social trends if they are to survive and/or be agents of social change in their cultures. Social trends and changing contexts also produce new ecclesial realities. Voluntarism is a key feature of religious life in Britain and North America and must be understood and accounted for in effective religious communities. Looking to the future, especially the next quarter century or so, the voluntary impulse will be felt.

One aspect of voluntarism that gives evidence of its energy and creates both new forms and anxiety is spontaneity. Anxiety results when low predictability of behaviour is perceived or where institutions are threatened. In religious organizations, spontaneity is exhibited when new leadership moves boldly in new directions and doesn't necessarily respect conventions or spend the requisite time to communicate and educate constituencies. Voluntarism is spontaneous, and therefore its exponents may behave in haste. Part of the poor reputation attributed to leaders of voluntarist organizations is that they lack the sophistication, skills, and knowledge to be leaders. Leaders may be catapulted to positions of influence beyond their immediate knowledge and capability and without due regard for those who may already be involved in a similar or identical work. For their part, voluntarists must increase the opportunities for leadership enhancement and take seriously the matter of leadership assessment.

Voluntarist theology must inevitably lead to a reconstruction of the doctrine of the Holy Spirit. Since much of Christian theological reflection emerges from experience, one can argue that this has in fact already begun. In a fragmented beginning with the charismatic movement and among the Vineyard Fellowships, spontaneous voluntary experience with the Spirit has led to a widespread revision of the doctrine of the Holy Spirit. The number and variety of literary works on the Holy Spirit have increased dramatically in the past decade. There is a hunger in the church for information on the person and experience of the Holy Spirit. What is needed for the larger church is a working doctrine of the Holy Spirit that gives continual

170

new life and calls forth unexpected new directions in leadership and mission, while always focussing on the timeless Christ. The Holy Spirit needs to be reclaimed by the church and honoured in the parachurch organizations. Parachurch and other forms of Christian voluntarism must be understood as "spiritual" ministries as certainly as ordained, ecclesiastically sanctioned ministries are. Churches must come to be open to critique and change and even desire it; associations must recognize the value of institutional integrity and exercise patience and grace as they attempt to modify behaviour. More emphasis should be placed upon those persons who serve both spheres — churches and the voluntary sector — to be consistent in their application of voluntarist principles and the unity of the Spirit within their associations and churchly contexts.

Also needed in the Christian community of the late twentieth and early twenty-first centuries is a new doctrine of the church that is inclusive and recognizes the sphere of many facets of endeavour. This new ecclesiology must emphasize the broadest possible engagement of laypersons as a positive contribution to the advancement of Christian objectives. "Lay empowerment" must become a specific objective of ministry and theological education. What the church considers to be its functions must be opened to include, with full acceptance and even celebration, the work of voluntary associations. Terminology in this regard is not unimportant. The terms "interdenominational" or "interecclesial" are preferable to "nondenominational" or "undenominational" or "transdenominational" because they stress the cooperative nature of voluntarist work and reduce the sense of organizational intimidation. The day of ecclesiastical turf exclusivism must pass!

The principles of sound pastoral theology should be applied to the relationships between churches and voluntary associations. Pastoral leaders are by nature supposed to be mediators and reconcilers of conflict, and this would seem to have direct application to working with diverse expressions of Christian action. Pastors need to emulate the shepherding models of Christ in bringing people together and seeking consensus. Rather than developing a competitive or hostile stance toward other forms of associations, church leaders need instead to look for ways of cooperating with and complementing

171

voluntary associations, creating new families or communities of fellowship and work. Partnership is a key strategy and relationship for the parishes of the immediate future, as Catholic pastoral theologians have discovered.[6] The church derives little benefit, and probably considerable harm, from evincing hostility to new participants or viable forms of Christian endeavour.

Effective pastoral leadership in the administrative and educational areas will be a key to managing and bringing effective results to congregations undergoing transition from large collectives to small groups. Pastors and lay leaders trained in nurture and empowerment of people in social settings of ten to twenty persons will likely enjoy a wider utility than those equipped only to manage large congregations. This will doubtless have a significant impact on preaching, witness, strategies for mission, and stewardship.[7] More proximate, relational forms of ministry will replace spectator congregations. The curricula of theological schools that are based implicitly on models of larger congregations must be revised to the social realities of the era.

Voluntary associations could be in jeopardy of losing their religious idealism or of making mistakes that have been long avoided by those with a longer Christian experience. As the organizational demands and government accountabilities for voluntary associations increase, there is a natural tendency to allow less definitive religious principles to define the association. For groups that cherish strongly defined doctrines or principles, this can mean a trend toward intolerable definitions. For other groups, it may mean the loss of specifically Christian ideals, as in the case of many of the YMCA chapters in the United States and Canada. Strong interaction between the church community and the life and work of associations can help to maintain clear ideals.

For their part, participants in voluntary associations must

6. Mary Benet McKinney, *Sharing Wisdom: A Process for Group Decision Making* (Valencia, Calif.: Tabor Publishing, 1987), and James D. Whitehead and Evelyn E. Whitehead, *The Promise of Partnership: Leadership and Ministry in an Adult Church* (San Francisco: Harper and Row, 1991).

7. Of the books on the impact of the small group on ministry, Loughlan Sofield and Brenda Hermann, *Developing the Parish as a Community of Service* (New York: Jesuit Educational Center, 1984), is useful from a Catholic perspective.

likewise support and celebrate the ancient and valued witness of the churches and their overall roles as part of the cultural landscape in which we live. The sacramental witness of the churches, their capacities to discern full-time leadership capabilities, their nurturing, pastoral functions, and their nature as intimate *koinonia* communities are all needful in the expeditious, objective-oriented voluntary sectors of Christian work.[8] Faithful membership of voluntarists in a local congregation and cooperative working arrangements with local churches, where appropriate, are important recognitions of the role of the churches. World Vision, by its declared objectives, and Inter-Varsity model this recognition and participation well. Great care is taken in these organizations to train staff persons with adequate theologies of the church and to require active participation in the life of the church.[9] It is inappropriate theologically and unhelpful in terms of ministry to assume that the institutional church will cease to be a major determinant in the future of Christianity.

A sure trend, with which Christians of all organizational kinds must reckon, is the increased scarcity of resources. Christian leaders, first in the churches, have begun to realize that there are limited financial and personnel resources available for religious purposes. Thus there is a critical need in the near future to reduce structures, expenditures, and assignments to the barest effective minimum. At the same time, new evangelistic and stewardship strategies and discipleship training must be given priority by churches and associations alike. Recent downturns in the benevolence economies of Britain and North American communities, with concomitant decreases in donations, demonstrate that no sector of the Christian

8. One writer has summarized the inabilities of voluntary associations to provide community and pastoral care: Charles J. Mellis, "Voluntary Societies as Communities: Insights from Rufus Anderson," *Missiology: An International Review* 6, no. 1 (January 1978): 95.

9. World Vision, for instance, asserts that it pursues its mission by serving the Church. See Purpose Statement for World Vision. InterVarsity has developed working papers, "Working Relationships" and "InterVarsity's Relationships to the Church and the Various Denominations Within the Church," that illustrate its care for a positive partnership. See also "IFES and the Church," *IFES ADMINISTRY* 1 (1990): 18, for an international perspective.

community is immune to these challenges. There is a significant wellspring of theological and organizational accomplishment upon which the entire Christian community could draw. A contemporary analysis of the primitive Christian context, as well as periods of widespread renewal, would be a useful starting point for redirection. To encourage faithful people to pursue the rewards of Christ as an end in themselves has proven its worth many times in Christian history.

In the final analysis, to Christian people who live in transition times — a "pilgrim people," to use John Bunyan's phrase — voluntarism must be seen in a positive light. Ultimately, spontaneous impulses in the life of a Christian believer or congregation are, more often than not, born of God. It is God who brings about change, initiates creativity, and empowers for new directions. Only God knows the future of the Christian movement, and only God can orient the church in the appropriate direction. Far from being destructive iconoclasm or "deconstructionism," or becoming a source of anxiety, the voluntarist impulse needs to be interpreted in light of the oracle of the seventh-century-B.C.E. Israelite prophet Habakkuk:

> Look at the nations, and see! Be astonished! Be astounded! For a work is being done in your days that you would not believe if you were told. (Hab. 1:5)

Bibliography

Biblical and Theological Backgrounds
of Religious Voluntarism

Bright, John. *A History of Israel.* Philadelphia: Westminster Press, 1959.

Bruce, F. F. *New Testament History.* Garden City, N.J.: Anchor Books, 1969.

De Vaux, Roland. *Ancient Israel.* New York: McGraw Hill, 1965.

Dill, Samuel. *Roman Society: From Nero to Marcus Aurelius.* New York: Meridian Books, 1956.

Erb, Peter, ed. *Pietists: Selected Writings.* New York: Paulist Press, 1983.

Frend, W. H. C. *The Rise of Christianity.* Philadelphia: Fortress Press, 1984.

Gilkey, Langdon. *Reaping the Whirlwind: A Christian Interpretation of History.* New York: Seabury Press, 1976.

Hayes, John H. *Understanding the Psalms.* Valley Forge, Pa.: Judson Press, 1976.

Jordan, W. K. *The Development of Religious Toleration in England, From the Convention of the Long Parliament to the Restoration 1640-1660.* Gloucester, Mass.: Peter Smith, 1965.

Pelikan, Jaroslav. *The Growth of Medieval Theology, 600-1300.* Chicago: University of Chicago Press, 1978.

Richardson, Alan. *An Introduction to the Theology of the New Testament.* New York: Harper and Row, 1958.

Rickaby, Joseph J. *Freewill and Four English Philosophers: Hobbes, Locke, Hume, and Mill.* Freeport, N.Y.: Books for Library Press, 1969.

Stambaugh, John, and David L. Balch. *The New Testament in Its Social Environment.* Philadelphia: Westminster Press, 1986.

Russell, David S. *From Early Judaism to Early Church.* Philadelphia: Fortress Press, 1986.

Van der Berg, J. *Constrained by Jesus' Name: An Inquiry into the Motives of the Missionary Awakening in Great Britain in the Period Between 1698 and 1815.* Kampen, The Netherlands: J. H. Kok, 1956.

Winter, Ralph D. "The Two Structures of God's Redemptive Mission." *Missiology: An International Review* (1974): 122-23.

The History and Development of Christian Voluntarism

A. Great Britain

Black, Eugene. *The Association: British Extraparliamentary Political Organization, 1769-1783.* Cambridge, Mass.: Harvard University Press, 1963.

Bowen, Desmond. *The Idea of the Victorian Church: A Study of the Church of England 1833-1889.* Montreal: McGill Queens University Press, 1968.

Brackney, William H. *Christian Voluntarism in Britain and North America: A Bibliography and Critical Assessment.* Westport, Conn.: Greenwood Press, 1995.

Bradley, Ian. *The Call to Seriousness: The Evangelical Impact on the Victorians.* London: Jonathan Cape, 1976.

Brown, Ford K. *Fathers of the Victorians: The Age of Wilberforce.* Cambridge: Cambridge University Press, 1961.

Bullock, F. W. B. *Voluntary Religious Societies 1520-1799.* St. Leonard's by the Sea: Budd and Gillatt, 1963.

Gilbert, A. D. *Religion and Society in Industrial England: Church, Chapel and Social Change, 1740-1914.* London: Longman, 1976.

Gosden, P. H. J. H. *Self-Help: Voluntary Associations in the Nineteenth Century.* London: T. Batson, 1973.

Heasman, Kathleen. *Evangelicals in Action: An Appraisal of Their Social Work in the Victorian Era.* London: Geoffrey Bles, 1962.

Hill, Christopher. *The World Turned Upside Down: Radical Ideas During the English Reformation.* London: Penguin Books, 1984.

Hilton, Boyd. *The Age of Atonement: The Influence of Evangelicalism on Social and Economic Thought, 1793-1865*. Oxford: Clarendon Press, 1988.

Lovegrove, Deryck N. *Established Church, Sectarian People: Itinerancy and the Transformation of English Dissent 1780-1830*. Cambridge: Cambridge University Press, 1988.

Martin, R. H. *Evangelicals United: Ecumenical Stirrings in Pre-Victorian Britain, 1795-1830*. Metuchen, N.J.: Scarecrow Press, 1983.

Mechie, Stewart. *The Church and Scottish Social Development, 1780-1870*. London: Oxford University Press, 1960.

Norman, E. R. *Church and Society in England 1770-1970: A Historical Study*. Oxford: Clarendon Press, 1976.

Walsh, John. "Theology of the Evangelical Revival." In *Essays in Modern English Church History*, edited by G. V. Bennett and J. Walsh. New York: Oxford University Press, 1966.

Ward, W. R. *Religion and Society in England, 1790-1850*. London: T. Batsford, 1972.

Watts, Michael. *The Dissenters: From the Reformation to the French Revolution*. Oxford: Clarendon Press, 1978.

Wright, Louis B. *Religion and Empire: The Alliance Between Piety and Commerce in English Expansionism, 1558-1625*. Chapel Hill, N.C.: University of North Carolina Press, 1943.

B. United States

Ahlstrom, Sydney E. *A Religious History of the American People*. New Haven, Conn.: Yale University Press, 1972.

Baird, Robert. *Religion in America, or an Account of the Origin, Relation to the State, and Recent Condition of the Evangelical Churches in the United States, with Notices of the Unevangelical Denominations*. New York: Harper Brothers, 1856.

Barnes, Gilbert H. *The Antislavery Impulse, 1830-1844*. New York: D. Appleton Century, 1933.

Bestor, Arthur. *Backwoods Utopias: The Sectarian Origins and the Owenite Phase of Communitarian Socialism in America 1663-1829*. Philadelphia: University of Pennsylvania Press, 1970.

BIBLIOGRAPHY

Billington, Ray A. *The Protestant Crusade: A Study of American Nativism.* New York: Macmillan, 1938.

Brackney, William H. *Voluntarism: The Dynamic Principle of the Free Church.* Wolfville, N.S.: Acadia University, 1991.

De Tocqueville, Alexis. *Democracy in America.* New York: Vintage Books, 1945.

Foster, Charles I. *An Errand of Mercy: The Evangelical United Front 1790-1837.* Chapel Hill, N.C.: University of North Carolina Press, 1960.

Goodykoontz, Colin B. *Home Missions on the American Frontier.* New York: Octagon Books, 1971.

Griffin, Clifford S. *Their Brother's Keepers: Moral Stewardship in the United States 1800-1865.* New Brunswick, N.J.: Rutgers University Press, 1960.

Handy, Robert T. *A Christian America: Protestant Hopes and Historical Realities.* New York: Oxford University Press, 1984.

Hatch, Nathan O. *The Democratization of American Christianity.* New Haven, Conn.: Yale University Press, 1989.

Hudson, Winthrop S. *American Protestantism.* Chicago: University of Chicago Press, 1967.

Marty, Martin. *Righteous Empire: The Protestant Experience in America.* New York: The Dial Press, 1970.

Mead, Sidney E. *The Lively Experiment: The Shaping of Christianity in America.* New York: Harper and Row, 1963.

Miyakawa, T. Scott. *Protestants and Pioneers: Individualism and Conformity on the American Frontier.* Chicago: University of Chicago Press, 1964.

Powell, Milton. *The Voluntary Church: American Religious Life (1740-1865) Seen Through the Eyes of European Visitors.* New York: Macmillan, 1967.

Schlesinger, Arthur M. "Biography of a Nation of Joiners." *American Historical Review* 50 (1944): 1-25.

Smith, Timothy L. *Revivalism and Social Reform in Mid-Nineteenth Century America.* New York: Abingdon Press, 1957.

Stokes, Anson P. *Church and State in the United States.* 3 vols. New York: Harper and Row, 1950.

Tewksbury, Donald G. *The Founding of American Colleges and Universities Before the Civil War.* New York: Teacher's College, Columbia University, 1932.

Tyler, Alice F. *Freedom's Ferment: Phases of American Social History from the Revolution to the Outbreak of the Civil War.* New York: Harper Torchbooks, 1962.

Wright, Conrad E. *The Transformation of Charity in Post-Revolutionary New England.* Boston: Northeastern University Press, 1992.

Wuthnow, Robert. *Faith and Philanthropy in America: Exploring the Role of Religion in America's Voluntary Sector.* San Francisco: Jossey-Bass, 1990.

————. *The Restructuring of American Religion: Society and Faith Since World War II.* Princeton, N.J.: Princeton University Press, 1988.

C. Canada

Bibby, Reginald W. *Fragmented Gods: The Poverty and Potential of Religion in Canada.* Toronto: Irwin Publishing Co., 1988.

Clark, S. D. *Church and Sect in Canada.* Toronto: University of Toronto Press, 1948.

Crail, James. *The Missionary Problem, Containing a History of Protestant Missions.* Toronto, Ont.: William Briggs, 1883.

Gibson, Theo T. *Robert Alexander Fyfe: His Contemporaries and His Influence.* Burlington, Ont.: Welch Publishing Co., 1988.

Grant, John Webster. *The Church in the Canadian Era.* Burlington, Ont.: Welch Publishing Co., 1988.

Mann, W. E. *Sect, Cult, and Church in Alberta.* Toronto: University of Toronto Press, 1955.

Moir, John S. *The Church in the British Era: From the British Conquest to Confederation.* Toronto: McGraw Hill Ryerson Press, 1971.

Rossides, D. W. *Voluntary Participation in Canada: A Comparative Analysis.* Toronto: York University, 1966.

Wilson, Alan. *The Clergy Reserves in Upper Canada.* Ottawa, Ont.: Canadian Historical Association, 1969.

Sociology and Religious Voluntarism

Gordon, C. Wayne, and Nicholas Babchuck. "A Typology of Voluntary Associations." *American Sociological Review* 24 (1959): 22-29.

Harrison, Paul M. *Authority and Power in the Free Church Tradition.* Princeton, N.J.: Princeton University Press, 1959.

Hassard, John, and Martin Parker, eds. *Postmodernism and Organizations.* London: Sage Publications, 1993.

Knudten, Richard D. *The Sociology of Religion: An Anthology.* New York: Appleton-Century-Crofts, 1967.

Lacoursiere, Roy B. *The Life Cycle of Groups: Group Developmental Stage Theory.* New York: Human Sciences Press, 1980.

Michels, Robert. *Political Parties: A Sociological Study of the Oligarchical Tendencies of Modern Democracy,* translated by Eden and Cedar Paul. New York: The Free Press, 1962.

Moberg, David O. *The Church as a Social Institution: The Sociology of American Religion.* Grand Rapids, Mich.: Baker Book House, 1984.

Robertson, D. B., ed. *Voluntary Associations: A Study of Groups in Free Societies: Essays in Honor of James Luther Adams.* Richmond, Va.: John Knox Press, 1966.

Rose, Arnold M. "Some Functions of Voluntary Associations." In *The Government of Associations: Selections from the Behavioral Sciences,* edited by William A. Glaser and David L. Sills. Totowa, N.J.: Bedminster Press, 1966.

Sills, David L. "Voluntary Associations — Sociological Aspects." In *International Encyclopedia of the Social Sciences,* edited by David L. Sills. New York: Macmillan, 1968.

Smith, David H. "The Importance of Formal Voluntary Association for Society." *Sociology and Social Research* 50 (1966): 483-94.

————. *Voluntary Action Research: 1972.* Lexington, Mass.: Lexington Books, 1972.

Wilson, Bryan R. *The Social Dimensions of Sectarianism: Sects and New Religious Movements in Contemporary Society.* Oxford: Clarendon Press, 1990.

Practical Applications: The Local Congregation, Parachurch Organizations, etc.

Allen, Roland. *The Spontaneous Expansion of the Church.* Grand Rapids, Mich.: Eerdmans, 1962.

Anderson, Leith. *Dying for Change: An Arresting Look at the New Realities Confronting Churches and Parachurch Ministries.* Minneapolis: Bethany House Publishers, 1991.

Apps, Gerald W. *Leadership for the Emerging Age: Transforming Practice in Adult and Continuing Education.* San Francisco: Jossey Bass, 1994.

Bolman, Lee G., and Terrance E. Deal. *Reframing Organizations: Artistry, Choice, and Leadership.* San Francisco: Jossey Bass, 1991.

Clegg, S. *Modern Organizations: Organization Studies in the Postmodern World.* London: Sage Books, 1990.

Craddock, Fred B. *Preaching.* Burlington, Ont.: Welch Publishing Co., 1991.

Evans, J. Claude. *Strategies of Deconstruction: Derrida and the Myth of the Voice.* Minneapolis: University of Minnesota Press, 1991.

Gremillion, Joseph, and Jim Castelli. *The Emerging Parish: The Notre Dame Study of Catholic Life Since Vatican II.* San Francisco: Harper and Row, 1987.

Hales, Edward J., and Alan J. Youngren. *Your Money/Their Ministry.* Grand Rapids, Mich.: Eerdmans, 1981.

Hall, Douglas J. *The Steward: A Biblical Symbol Come of Age.* New York: Friendship Press, 1982.

Mellis, Charles J. "Voluntary Societies as Communities." *Missiology: An International Review* 6:1 (January 1978): 91-96.

Niebuhr, H. Richard, and Daniel Day Williams. *The Ministry in Historical Perspective.* New York: Harper and Row, 1982.

Oden, Thomas C. *Pastoral Theology: Essentials of Ministry.* San Francisco: Harper and Row, 1983.

Snyder, Howard. *The Problem of Wineskins.* Downers Grove, Ill.: InterVarsity Press, 1975.

Steinbron, Melvin. *Can the Pastor Do It Alone?* Ventura, Calif.: Regal Books, 1987.

Tan, Siang-Yang. *Lay Counseling: Equipping Christians for a Helping Ministry.* Grand Rapids, Mich.: Zondervan Publishing Co., 1991.

BIBLIOGRAPHY

Tillapaugh, Frank R. *The Church Unleashed.* Ventura, Calif.: Regal Books, 1982.

Tucker, Ruth A., and Walter Liefeld. *Daughters of the Church: Women and Ministry from New Testament Times to the Present.* Grand Rapids, Mich.: Zondervan Publishing House, 1987.

Vallet, Ronald E. *Stepping Stones of the Steward: A Faith Journey Through Jesus' Parables,* 5th ed. Grand Rapids, Mich.: Eerdmans and Manlius, N.Y.: REV/Rose Publishing, 1994.

————, and Charles E. Zech. *The Mainline Church's Funding Crisis: Issues and Possibilities.* Grand Rapids, Mich.: Eerdmans and Manlius, N.Y.: REV/Rose Publishing, 1995.

White, Jerry. *The Church and Parachurch: An Uneasy Marriage.* Portland, Ore.: Multnomah Press, 1983.

Whitehead, James D., and Evelyn Eaton Whitehead. *The Promise of Partnership: Leadership and Ministry in an Adult Church.* San Francisco, Calif.: Harper and Row, 1991.

Winter, Ralph D. "Protestant Mission Societies: The American Experience." *Missiology: An International Review* 7:2 (1979): 139-78.

Wuthnow, Robert. *"I Come Away Stronger": How Small Groups Are Shaping American Religion.* Grand Rapids, Mich.: Eerdmans, 1994.

Index

INDEX

Index

185

INDEX

INDEX

Humane Society, 44
Human freedom, 49
Humanitarian voluntarism, 77, 81, 121, 142
Humbard, Rex, 78
Hymn Society of the United States and Canada, 77
Hyperaspistes, 31

Ideological constraint, 126
Imago dei, 24
Incipient phase, 86
Income tax codes, 155
Independent missions, 169
Independents, 53
Indian missions, 76
Institute of Christian Sociology, 76
Institutional Church League, 74, 76
Intercollegiate Christian Union, 63
Inter-Collegiate Gospel Fellowship, 141
Interdenominational voluntarism, 72-74, 171
International Missionary Council, 65, 101
InterVarsity Christian Fellowship, 137, 141, 173
InterVarsity Fellowship of Evangelical Unions, 141
Interweave, 79
Isaiah, the prophet, 12
Itinerant evangelism, 59
Itinerant Society, 91
Ivimey, Joseph, 92

Jeremiah, the prophet, 12
Jesus of Nazareth, 14
Jesus People, 123
Jewish missions, 63-64
Jews, 37
John the Baptizer, 14, 18
Jones, Larry, 143

Judson, Adoniram, 73
Julian of Eclanum, 27

Keswick Convention, 62, 63, 99, 141
King, Charles, 63
King James Version, 98
Knights of Columbus, 120
Knights of St. John, 82
Koinonia, 133, 173
Ku Klux Klan, 75

Ladies' circles, 160
Language classes, 154
Last Rites, 149
Lausanne Committee, 88
Lausanne Movement, 88-89
Lausanne II, 89
Law, William, 43
Lay empowerment, 171
Leadership development, 139, 168-69
League of Evangelical Students, 141
Lebanon Nurses Association, 64
Lee, Luther, 103
Legters, L. L., 99
Lesbian and Gay Christian Movement, 65
Letter on Toleration, 36
Liberal Methodism, 104
Life cycle of organizations, 85-90, 136-37
Lightfoot, J. B., 63
Locke, John, 34-37, 43, 49
Lockport Conference, Methodist Church, 104
London Missionary Society, 60, 61, 96
London Tavern, 95
Lord's Day Alliance, 77; in Canada, 81
Lord's Supper, 150
Luther, Martin, 31-33, 149